EGERTON RYERSON AND EDUCATION IN UPPER CANADA

First published 1912
This edition published by Lector House in 2024

ISBN: 978-93-6138-828-6

Lector House LLP
Registered Office: H. No. 96, Block C, Tomar Colony,
Burari, Delhi – 110084, India
info@lectorhouse.com
www.lectorhouse.com

EGERTON RYERSON AND EDUCATION IN UPPER CANADA

JOHN HAROLD PUTMAN

2024

LECTOR HOUSE

LECTOR HOUSE LLP

EGERTON RYERSON AND EDUCATION IN UPPER CANADA

BY

J. HAROLD PUTMAN, B.A., D.PAED.,

Inspector of Public Schools, Ottawa, Ont.

(Formerly in charge of the Departments in Psychology and English, Ottawa Normal School)

PREFACE.

The object of this volume is to give a succinct idea of the nature and history of our Ontario School Legislation. This legislation is so bound up with the name of Egerton Ryerson that to give its history is to relate the work of his life.

It would be useless to attempt to show how our school legislation developed under Responsible Government without some understanding of its history previous to the time of Ryerson. I have, therefore, devoted three chapters to a brief account of education in Upper Canada previous to 1844.

No attempt has been made to give the history of our schools since Ryerson's retirement, partly because no radical changes have been made, and partly because it would involve criticism of statesmen and teachers who are still actively engaged in work. Nor has any attempt been made to trace the history of University education after 1845. To do so would require a complete volume. But, as University education prior to 1844 was so closely connected with Common and Grammar Schools, it seemed necessary, up to a certain point, to trace the course of all three together.

The introductory chapter on the biography of Ryerson is only indirectly connected with the other chapters, and may be omitted by the reader who has no interest in the man himself.

It is hoped that this volume may encourage teachers in service and teachers in training to acquire a fuller knowledge of their own educational institutions.

THE AUTHOR.

OTTAWA, July 1st, 1912.

CONTENTS

EGERTON RYERSON AND EDUCATION IN UPPER CANADA.

CHAPTER I.

BIOGRAPHICAL.

Egerton Ryerson was born in 1803, in the township of Charlotteville, now a part of the county of Norfolk. His father was a United Empire Loyalist who had held some command in a volunteer regiment of New Jersey. After the Revolution the elder Ryerson settled first in New Brunswick, coming later to Upper Canada, where he took up land and became a pioneer farmer. The young Ryersons, of whom there were several, took their full share in the laborious farm work, and Egerton seems to have prided himself upon his physical strength and his skill in all farm operations.

He received such an education as was afforded by the indifferent Grammar School of the London District, supplemented by the reading of whatever books he could secure.

At an early age he was strongly drawn toward that militant Christianity preached by the early Methodist Circuit Riders, and at the age of eighteen joined the Methodist Society. This step created an estrangement between Ryerson and his father, who already had two sons in the Methodist ministry. Ryerson left home and became usher in the London District Grammar School, where he remained two years, when his father sent for him to come home. After some further farming experience, the young man went to Hamilton to attend the Gore District Grammar School. He was already thinking of becoming a Methodist preacher, and wished to prepare himself by a further course of study. During his stay in Hamilton under the instruction of John Law, he worked so eagerly at Latin and Greek that he fell ill of a fever which nearly ended his career.

When barely twenty-two years of age he decided to travel as a Methodist missionary.

In a letter written about this time to his brother, the Rev. George Ryerson, we get a glimpse of the young preacher's ideas upon the preparation of sermons. "On my leisure days I read from ten to twenty verses of Greek a day besides reading history, the Scriptures, and the best works on practical divinity, among which Chalmers has decidedly the preference in my mind both for piety and depth of thought. These two last studies employ the greatest part of my time. My preaching is altogether original. I endeavour to collect as many ideas from every source as I can; but I do not copy the expression of anyone, for I do detest seeing blooming flowers in dead men's hands. I think it my duty and I try to get a general knowledge and view of any subject that I discuss beforehand; but not unfrequently I have tried to preach with only a few minutes' previous reflection."[1]

After being received into the Methodist connection as a probationer, Ryerson was assigned a charge on Yonge St., which embraced the town of York and several adjacent townships. It took four weeks on horseback and on foot over almost impassable roads to complete the circuit. During this time the probationer was expected to conduct from twenty-five to thirty-five services. The accommodation furnished by the pioneers was of the rudest kind, but the people gave the travelling preacher a hearty welcome. Young Ryerson was acquainting himself with conditions in Upper Canada at first hand by living among the people. At a later time, when the opportunity came, he made use of his intimate knowledge to secure for these people the advantages of better schools.

During this first year of his missionary ministry, Ryerson was drawn into the Clergy Reserves controversy. The Methodist Society in Upper Canada was an offshoot of that body in the United States. This connection had come about in a very natural way. Upper Canada was largely settled by United Empire Loyalists. The Methodist circuit-riders naturally followed their people into the wilds of Upper Canada. In many districts no religious services of any kind were held except those of the Methodists.

In May, 1826, a pamphlet was published, being a sermon preached by Archdeacon Strachan, of York, on the occasion of the death of the Bishop of Quebec. This pamphlet contained an historical sketch of the rise and progress of the Anglican Church in Canada. The claim was made that the Anglican Church was by law the Established Church of Upper Canada. The Methodists were singled out and held up to ridicule. They were represented as American and disloyal. Their preachers were declared to be ignorant and spreaders of sedition, and the Imperial Parliament was petitioned to grant £300,000 a year to the Anglican Church in Canada to enable it to maintain the loyalty of Upper Canada to Britain.

To Ryerson, the son of a Loyalist, this was more than could be borne, and he immediately crossed swords with the Anglican prelate by writing a defence of Methodism and calling into question the exclusive demands made by Strachan on behalf of the Anglicans. The contest waxed warm and then hot. The whole country was convulsed. Within four years the Legislature of Upper Canada passed Acts allowing the various religious denominations to hold lands for churches, parsonages, and burying-grounds, and also allowing their ministers to solemnize marriages. Besides these concessions, the Legislative Assembly was forced by public opinion to petition the Imperial Parliament against the claims of the Anglican Church to be an Established Church in Canada and to a monopoly of the Clergy Reserves.

[1] See "Story of My Life," by Ryerson, edited by Hodgins, page 42.

During his second year in the ministry, Ryerson spent part of his time on a mission to the Chippewa Indians on the Credit River. While there, he showed himself to be very practical. He encouraged the Indians to build better houses and to clear and cultivate the land.[2] "After having collected the means necessary to build the house of worship and schoolhouse, I showed the Indians how to enclose and make gates for their gardens. Between daylight and sunrise I called out four of the Indians in succession and showed them how, and worked with them, to clear and fence in, and plow and plant their first wheat and corn fields. In the afternoon I called out the schoolboys to go with me and cut and pile and burn the underbrush in and around the village. The little fellows worked with great glee as long as I worked with them, but soon began to play when I left them."

A letter written by Rev. William Ryerson to his brother, the Rev. George Ryerson, on March 8th, 1827, after a visit to the Indian Mission, shows Egerton Ryerson's practical nature and incidentally gives us his method of instruction. "I visited Egerton at the Credit last week. . . . They have about forty pupils on the list, but there were only thirty present. The rest were absent making sugar. . . . Their progress in spelling, reading, and writing, is astonishing, but especially in writing, which certainly exceeds anything I ever saw. When I was there they were fencing the lots in the village in a very neat, substantial manner. On my arrival at the Mission I found Egerton, about half a mile from the village, stripped to the shirt and pantaloons, clearing land with between twelve and twenty of the little Indian boys, who were all engaged in chopping and picking up the brush."[3]

At the Methodist Conference of 1827, Ryerson was sent to the Cobourg Circuit. During his term there he was again drawn into a controversy with Dr. Strachan, who sent to the Imperial Parliament an Ecclesiastical Chart, purporting to give an account of religion in Upper Canada. Ryerson claimed that this chart contained many false statements and that it was peculiarly unfair to the Methodists. The real point at issue was whether the Anglican Church was to become the Established Church of Upper Canada.

In 1828, Ryerson was appointed to the Hamilton and Ancaster Circuit, which reached from within five miles of Brantford to Stoney Creek. On September 10th, 1828, he married Hannah Aikman, of Hamilton.[4]

The Methodist Conference of 1829 determined to establish an official newspaper to be known as *The Christian Guardian*. Ryerson was elected as the first editor and was sent to New York to procure the plant. The paper started with a circulation of 500, which in three years was increased to some 3,000. Besides defending Methodist principles and institutions, the paper made a strong stand for civil liberty, temperance, education, and missionary work. It soon came to be looked upon as one of the leading journals of Upper Canada. Ryerson gave up the position of editor in 1832, and the following year made a trip to England to negotiate a union between the Canadian Methodist Conference and the Wesleyan Conference of England. The union was consummated. Ryerson returned to Canada and was

[2] See "Story of My Life," by Egerton Ryerson, edited by Hodgins, page 60.

[3] See "Story of My Life," page 69.

[4] Died in 1832. In 1833, Ryerson married Mary Armstrong, of Toronto.

re-elected editor of the *Guardian*.

While in England, he had interviews with Earl Ripon, Lord Stanley and other public men, to whom he gave valuable information concerning Canadian affairs, especially those connected with the vexed question of the status of the Anglican Church.

On his return to Canada, in 1833, Ryerson published in the *Guardian* "Impressions Made by My Late Visit to England." In this article he gave his estimate of Tories, Whigs, and Radicals. He saw much to admire in the moderate Tories, little to praise in the Whigs, and much to condemn in the Radicals. His strictures on the latter called down upon him the wrath and invective of William Lyon Mackenzie. To some extent Ryerson's articles led the constitutional reformers in Upper Canada to separate themselves from those reformers who were prepared to establish a republican form of government in order to secure equal political and civil rights. To many of his old friends it seemed that Ryerson had given up championing liberty and had become a Tory. Many were ready to accuse him of self-seeking in his desire to conciliate the party of privilege. One reverend brother,[5] writing to him, says: "I can only account for your strange and un-Ryersonian conduct and advice on one principle—that there is something ahead which you, through your superior political spy-glass, have discovered and thus shape your course, while we landlubbers, short-sighted as we are, have not even heard of it." Hundreds of subscribers gave up the *Guardian* as a protest against the views of its editor, but as the crisis approached which culminated in the Rebellion of '37 and '38, the tide of public opinion turned in Ryerson's favour.

In 1835, Ryerson gave up the *Guardian* and took a church at Kingston. Scarcely was he settled when he undertook a second visit to England. The Methodists had, in 1832, laid the corner-stone of the Upper Canada Academy at Cobourg. They had no charter, although an unsuccessful attempt had been made to have the Trustee Board incorporated by the Legislature of Upper Canada. Extensive buildings were under way and the trustees were in financial difficulties. Ryerson was sent to England to beg subscriptions and also to attempt to secure a Royal Charter. The work was distasteful to him, but he persevered, and after more than a year and six months spent in England he accomplished three ends. He secured enough money in subscriptions to relieve the most pressing immediate needs of the Trustee Board. He secured an order from the Colonial Secretary directed to the Governor of Upper Canada, authorizing him to pay to the Upper Canada Academy, from the unappropriated revenues of the Crown, the sum of £4,000.[6] Last, and most important, he secured a Royal Charter, although up to that time no such charter had ever been issued to any religious body except the Established Church. To Ryerson, the visit to England was of prime importance. It gave him a broadened view of British institutions and English public men. It gave him a political experience that was of great value to him in later years. It gave him an opportunity to appeal to his fellow men upon the subject of education and educational institutions.

While in England, Ryerson contributed a series of letters to the London *Times*

[5] Rev. Jas. Evans, of Niagara District. See part of letter in "Story of My Life," page 131.

[6] Later, in 1837, Ryerson secured this money only after a petition to the Legislature.

on Canadian affairs. There was a prevalent feeling in England that a very large part of the Upper Canadian people was determined upon a republican form of government. Ryerson's letters did something to remove this impression.

After the Rebellion of 1837 was crushed, the constitutional reform party was apparently without any influence. It seemed that the Family Compact oligarchy would have everything in their own hands. Prospects for equality of civil and religious liberty were not bright, and it is significant of the Methodists' appreciation of Ryerson's ability that they immediately planned to make him again editor of the *Guardian*. His brother John, writing to him in March, 1838, said: "It is a great blessing that Mackenzie and radicalism are down, but we are in imminent danger of being brought under the domination of a military and high-church oligarchy which would be equally bad, if not infinitely worse. Under the blessing of Providence, there is one remedy and only one: that is for you to take the editorship of the *Guardian* again."[7]

Ryerson did take the position, and in his first editorial in the *Guardian* of the 11th July, 1838, says: "Notwithstanding the almost incredible calumny which has in past years been heaped upon me by antipodes-party-presses, I still adhere to the principles and views upon which I set out in 1826. I believe the endowment of the priesthood of any Church in the Province to be an evil to that church. . . . I believe that the appropriation of the proceeds of the Clergy Reserves to general educational purposes will be the most satisfactory and advantageous disposal of them that can be made. In nothing is this Province so defective as in the requisite available provisions for an efficient system of general education. Let the distinctive character of that system be the union of public and private effort. . . . To Government influence will be spontaneously added the various and combined religious influences of the country in the noble, statesmanlike and divine work of raising up an elevated, intelligent, and moral population."

Dr. Ryerson clearly saw that religion, politics, and education could not at this period be separated, and for the next two years he did his utmost, through the *Guardian*, to prevent the Anglican Church from securing undivided possession of the Clergy Reserves. The difficulties of his task were increased by the fact that there were in Canada several British Wesleyan missionaries who were not unwilling to see an Anglican Establishment. They were cleverly used by some of the Anglicans and their friends to cause ferment and sow discord among the Methodists in Canada. From 1838 until 1840, when he finally gave up the editorship of the *Guardian*, Ryerson fought strongly for equal religious privileges for all the people of Upper Canada. Nor were Ryerson's efforts in this direction confined to the columns of the *Guardian*. He addressed several communications to the new Colonial Secretary, Lord Normanby.

Lord Durham and his successor, Lord Sydenham, received the cordial support of Ryerson in their efforts to give a constitutional government to Canada. Largely through Ryerson's suggestion there was issued at Toronto, in 1841, the *Monthly Review*, which was to be a medium for disseminating the liberal views of Sydenham. Ryerson wrote the prospectus and contributed some articles. Probably as a

[7] See copy of letter in "Story of My Life," page 200.

recognition for this work, Sydenham sent him a draft for £100, which he promptly returned.

In May, 1840, Ryerson paid a fraternal visit to the American General Conference at Baltimore. At this time he fully purposed to take a church in New York City for one or two years. He even thought it quite possible that he might make the United States his permanent home. On his return to Canada from the Baltimore visit he was elected Secretary of the Conference. Charges were made against him by a British Wesleyan which determined him to visit England. This visit led to a rupture between the Canadian and British Methodist Conferences. When Ryerson and his brother returned to Canada, a special meeting of the Canada Conference was convened to consider the break with British Methodism. The result was a rupture in the Canadian Wesleyan Conference itself. Many blamed the Ryersons for the quarrel with the English Conference, and Egerton again thought seriously of going to the United States or of withdrawing from ministerial work. The truth seems to be that Ryerson was more than a preacher. He lived in stirring times, when the nascent elements of constitutional government were in process of crystallization. He unconsciously felt that he must have a part in directing the destinies of his native country. He saw clearly that the Canadian Methodist Church must ultimately be independent and that its ministers ought not to adopt a policy dictated to them by the English Conference, many members of which were wholly ignorant of Canadian conditions.

During the next two years, 1841 and 1842, Ryerson was in charge of the Adelaide Street Church, Toronto. He seems to have given himself up wholly to his pastoral work and to have taken little active part in passing events.

On the 27th of August, 1841, Lord Sydenham signed a bill which made Upper Canada Academy a college, with university powers. The name was changed to Victoria College. In October of the same year, Ryerson was appointed the first principal of the new college. He did not give up his church work until June, 1842. On the 21st of that month he was formally installed in his new position. On the 3rd of August the Wesleyan University of Middletown, Conn., conferred upon him the degree of Doctor of Divinity.

Lord Sydenham died in 1841. It seems that shortly before his death he had some communication with Ryerson regarding the latter's appointment as Superintendent of Education for Upper Canada. Ryerson claimed that the Governor actually promised him the appointment but that there had never been any official written record. Sydenham was succeeded by Sir Charles Bagot, who in May, 1842, made the Rev. Mr. Murray Superintendent of Education. Sir Charles Bagot died in May, 1843, and was succeeded by Sir Charles Metcalfe. It was a critical period in the history of Canada. The people were supposed to be in possession of the enjoyment of responsible government. But as a matter of fact, very few had any definite ideas as to what was meant by responsible government. Lord Metcalfe refused to accept the advice of his Council regarding an appointment. Instead of resigning at once as a protest they attempted to secure from him a promise that he would in future accept their recommendations. He refused. Later the leading members of the Council resigned. Party feeling ran high, and the Governor had few friends.

Ryerson had been upon familiar terms with Lord Durham, Lord Sydenham, and Sir Charles Bagot. He now had several communications and one or more interviews with Lord Metcalfe. He made direct and positive offers of his services to the Governor. He then wrote a series of nine letters in vindication of the Governor's course. These letters caused much excitement and won for Ryerson the lasting enmity of the advanced Reform party, who openly accused him of toadyism and of selling his support to Lord Metcalfe in return for the promise of office. Whatever may have been the effect of Ryerson's letters, Lord Metcalfe's party won a temporary victory and Ryerson himself was appointed Superintendent of Education for Upper Canada in October, 1844.

To show how the political opponents of Lord Metcalfe viewed Ryerson's appointment, the circumstances connected with it and his fitness for the position of Superintendent, I quote from the Toronto *Globe*, the editor of which was an out-and-out opponent of Ryerson and an unsparing critic of his early educational legislation. In the *Globe* of May 28th, 1844, there appeared a letter signed "Junius," protesting against Ryerson's appointment. The writer insinuates that Ryerson was won over by receiving some notice from Lord Metcalfe, and that the Governor hoped by winning over Ryerson to win a united support from the Methodists. He calls Ryerson a violent political partisan and taunts him with having only a superficial education. He says: "Nor is it flattering to the many learned men of the country that one represented to be of slender attainments in a few common branches of English education, and totally ignorant of mathematics and classics, should be entrusted with the education of the country, many of whose youthful scholars have attained higher knowledge than their chief."

In a *Globe* editorial of June 4th, 1844, in commenting upon Ryerson's first letter in defence of Lord Metcalfe, the writer says: "If the Rev. Mr. Ryerson's appearance in the political field is indecorous and uncalled for, the manner in which he has begun his work is in perfect keeping with that appearance. A more presumptuous and egotistical exhibition from a man of talents and education has never been brought under the public eye. The first column alone of his Address [preface to letters in defence of Lord Metcalfe] contains fifty repetitions of the little insignificant word *I*, to say nothing of *me* and *my*. . . . We may be permitted to express our utter astonishment, however, to find a minister of the Gospel embarking with so much eagerness in the sea of politics."

That Ryerson had a very good understanding with Lord Metcalfe as to the position of Superintendent of Education before writing the famous letters is apparent to anyone who reads the correspondence. That there was anything discreditable to either party in that understanding has never been shown. On the contrary, it seems quite certain that Ryerson honestly believed the Governor was right. It is certain he made out a strong case and likely won many supporters for the Metcalfe party. This was especially galling to the party who called themselves *Reformers*, because they had looked upon Ryerson as one of their champions. But Ryerson never had been, and never became, a mere party man. He fought for great principles, and if up to 1844 he had generally found himself with the Reformers, it was because they were championing what Ryerson believed to be the right.

To taunt him with being half-educated was the mark of a small mind. Every man must be judged according to the way he makes use of his opportunities, and by such a standard no man in Canadian public life has ever measured higher than Egerton Ryerson. He may have known "little Latin and less Greek," he may have been wholly ignorant of the binomial theorem, and he may not have been able to write as smooth and graceful English as the classical scholars of Oxford, but he knew that thousands of boys and girls in the backwoods of Upper Canada were growing up in ignorance; he knew that the secondary schools of Upper Canada were scarcely more efficient than they had been thirty years before, and he knew that the country had ample resources to give reasonable educational advantages to all. More than this, he must have felt that, given reasonable freedom and support, he could in a short time change the whole system of education.

Dr. Ryerson, in accepting appointment, stipulated that he should be allowed to make a tour of Europe before taking up the active duties of his office. He left Canada for Europe in November, 1844, and returned in December, 1845. He made an elaborate report[8] based on personal investigation into the schools of Great Britain and Ireland, France, Holland, Germany, Switzerland, and other European countries, besides New York and the New England States. Perhaps the systems of Ireland, Germany, and Massachusetts gave Ryerson more practical suggestions than those of any other countries. In Prussia he saw the advantages of trained teachers and a strong central bureau of administration; in Ireland he saw a simple solution of religious difficulties and a fine system of national textbooks; in Massachusetts he saw an efficient system managed by popularly elected boards of trustees.

During his absence Ryerson was again attacked and held up to ridicule by the *Globe*. In an editorial of April 29th, 1845,[9] we find the following: "The vanity of the Deputy Superintendent of Education demands fresh incense at every turn. He has doffed the politician for the moment and now comes out a ruling pedagogue of Canada. What a pity that he was not a cardinal or at least a stage representative of one! At what a rate would he strut upon the boards as Wolsey and rant for the benefit of his hearers and for his own benefit more especially! He beats all the presumptuous meddling priests of the day. . . . Doubtless the Rev. Mr. Ryerson is preparing to astonish the world by his educational researches in Europe and the United States. It will be a subject of no small amusement to watch his pranks. We shall no doubt hear of his visiting all the most celebrated Continental schools and are astonished he did not call at Oxford and Cambridge. He could no doubt have given them some excellent hints!"

In a *Globe* editorial of December 16th, 1845, when the Draper University Bill of that year was yet a topic of public discussion, we find this reference to Ryerson: "It is now more than twelve months since the Province was insulted by the appointment of Dr. Ryerson to the responsible situation of Superintendent of Public Instruction. To hide the gross iniquity of the transaction, Ryerson was sent out of the country on pretence of inquiring into the different systems of education. After being several months in England this public officer, paid by the people of Canada,

[8] See Chapter V.

[9] See bound volumes of *Globe* in Legislative Library, Toronto.

has for the last eight months been on the Continent on a tour of pleasure. . . . Let the people of Canada rejoice and every Methodist willing to be sold throw up his cap. Ryerson is here ready to dispose of them to the highest bidder, the purchase money to be applied to his own benefit with a modicum for Victoria College."

Ryerson's report of 1846 was favourably received, and the Government asked him to draft a school bill based on his report. This he did, and the Bill of 1846 became the basis of our Common School system. After Lord Metcalfe's departure from Canada and the election of a Reform administration, there was a clamour from strong party men that Ryerson should be removed. The Toronto *Globe* led in the attacks against him. It is a tribute to his ability and to the system of education which he proposed, that these attacks all failed and that Dr. Ryerson came by degrees to command the confidence of both political parties.

As soon as possible after his return from Europe in 1845, Ryerson moved from Cobourg to Toronto. When appointed in 1844, his rank was that of Deputy or Assistant Superintendent of Education for Upper Canada, the nominal head of the Department being the Provincial Secretary. The School Bill of 1846 made a change, and on June 17th of that year Ryerson received his commission as Superintendent of Education. One of his first acts was a proposal to found a journal of education, which should be a semi-official means of communication between the Superintendent on the one hand and District Superintendents, Trustees, Municipal Councillors, and teachers on the other. The "Journal" was established in 1848 and regularly issued until Ryerson gave up office in 1876.

In the autumn of 1847, Ryerson spent nearly three months visiting County School Conventions, where he explained the new School Act and delivered a lecture upon "The Importance of Education to an Agricultural People." In 1850, Ryerson began a struggle for free schools which lasted until 1871. About the same time he obtained permission from the Legislature to establish an Educational Depository in connection with the Education Department. He visited Europe and some American cities and made very advantageous arrangements for securing in large quantities books, maps, globes, and other school appliances. These were supplied to School Boards at 50 cents on the dollar. The Depository was continued in operation until 1881 and handled in all $1,000,000 worth of supplies. In 1853 Ryerson spent three months in attending County Conventions and addressed thirty meetings. During this tour he visited his native county of Norfolk, and at Simcoe was presented with an address by the School Board. On his return to Toronto he was presented with an address and a silver tea service by the officials of the Education Department and the teachers of the Normal School.

In 1853, Ryerson took advantage of an annual grant made by the Legislature in 1850 to establish public libraries throughout the Province. Before the end of 1855 no less than 117,000 volumes were distributed. In 1854 Ryerson was one of the Commissioners to prepare a report on a system of education for New Brunswick. In June, 1855, being in poor health, he got leave of absence to travel in Europe and to purchase objects of art for an educational museum. He was appointed Honorary Commissioner to the Paris Exposition by the Government. During his tour he visited London, spent several weeks in Paris, and made brief visits to Antwerp,

Brussels, Munich, Florence, and Rome.

In 1857, a new system of audit was adopted by the Government. Previous to this time the total money voted for schools for Upper Canada had been paid over to Ryerson. He gave bondsmen as security for the money and deposited it in the Toronto banks. Interest allowed on unexpended balances was credited to his personal account. This system seems to have been universal among officers in charge of public money at that time. But in 1857 the new auditor called in question Ryerson's right to this interest. After much wrangling, Ryerson paid over to the Government £1,375, being the amount he had received for interest. He then put in a claim of about the same amount for his expenses to Europe in 1844, and for amounts paid a deputy during his absence. The Government paid his claim, thus showing that they believed him morally entitled to the interest which he had repaid.

In 1860, Ryerson made a three months' educational tour, addressing County Conventions. In all, he attended thirty-five meetings, giving addresses on the subjects of "Vagrant Children," "Free Schools," and "Public Grammar Schools." He was given a public dinner by the teachers of Northumberland and Durham on the occasion of his official visit to Cobourg. In 1866 he made a similar tour, addressing forty meetings in seven weeks. His chief object was to create public opinion in favor of legislation on compulsory attendance, public libraries and township Boards of Trustees. Later in the same year he again got permission to visit Europe for the purpose of adding to the museum and collecting information on schools for the deaf, dumb, and blind. He visited New York, London, Paris, Rome, Venice, and Geneva, returning in 1867. On his return he presented to the Legislature an elaborate report on education in Great Britain and European countries. In December, 1868, Ryerson tendered his resignation, suggesting that a responsible Minister of Education should be appointed and proposing that he himself should be superannuated. The resignation was not accepted.

In 1869 he held another series of County Conventions. In the same year he wrote a letter to the Provincial Secretary, Hon. M. C. Cameron, reflecting on the action of Treasurer E. B. Wood in regard to a proposed change in the financial management of the Education Department. Ryerson's letter was indiscreet and would have led to his dismissal had he not withdrawn it. In 1872 the long-smouldering dissatisfaction of the Reform party with Ryerson's administration came to a head. The Honourable Edward Blake was Premier, and his Government disallowed some of Ryerson's regulations, questioned the authority of the Council of Public Instruction, and sought in many ways to curtail the Superintendent's power. Ryerson showed very little desire for conciliation and wished to refer the dispute to the Courts. He had so long and so successfully wielded an arbitrary power that he could not acquiesce in the system which made his Department subordinate to a responsible Cabinet. In 1873, Oliver Mowat became Attorney-General, and he, too, found Ryerson obdurate. Finally, as a result of this agitation, the Council of Public Instruction came to be composed partly of members elected by various bodies of teachers and partly by members appointed by the Cabinet. These latter were not recommended by the Superintendent, as had formerly been the custom. Friction over the Council continued during 1874 and 1875.

In 1876, Ryerson was retired on his full salary of $4,000 a year. The following May he went to England to consult documents in the library of the British Museum bearing on his work, "The Loyalists of America." He enjoyed fairly good health until within a few months of his death, which occurred on February 19th, 1882. The Government recognized his valuable services by a grant of $10,000 to his widow. On the 24th of May, 1889, a statue to his memory was unveiled on the grounds of the Education Department, the scene of his labours for nearly forty years.

CHAPTER II.

EDUCATION IN UPPER CANADA FROM 1783 TO 1844.

Immediately after the signing of the Treaty of Versailles in 1783, United Empire Loyalists began to make homes in Upper Canada. The Great Lakes and larger rivers were the natural highways. It happened, therefore, that the earliest settlements were along the St. Lawrence, the Niagara, and Lakes Erie and Ontario.

For a few years these settlers were too busy to think very much about schools. Man's first wants are food, clothing, and shelter. But just as soon as rude homes were built and a patch of forest cleared upon which to grow grain and vegetables, these Upper Canadian Loyalists began to think of schools. It was natural that they should do so. They were descendants of an intelligent stock, people who had good schools in New England and of a people whose forefathers had enjoyed liberal educational advantages in the old world.

Governor Simcoe reached Upper Canada in 1792, and almost immediately took steps to establish schools. He was an aristocrat who firmly believed in such a constitution of society as then existed in the old world. He naturally wished to see a reproduction of that society in the new world. Hence we are not surprised to find that his educational schemes were intended for the classes rather than for the masses. In a letter[10] written by Simcoe, April 28th, 1792, to the British Secretary of State, he urges grants of £100 each for schools at Niagara and Kingston. He also proposed a university with English Church professors.

In 1797, the House of Assembly and Legislative Council adopted an address to the King praying him to set apart waste lands of the Crown for the establishment of a respectable grammar school in each District, and also for a college or university. In answer to this petition, the Duke of Portland wrote saying that His Majesty proposed to comply with the request and wished further advice as to the best means of carrying it out.

The Executive Council, the Judges and law officers of the Crown met in consultation in 1798 and recommended that 500,000 acres of waste Crown lands be set apart to build a provincial university, and a free grammar school in each of the four Districts. Grammar schools were to be built at once at Kingston and at Niagara, and, as soon as circumstances would permit, at Cornwall and at Sandwich. The university was to be at York. It was estimated that each grammar school would cost £3,000 to build and £180 a year to maintain. The schools were to accommodate

[10] See D. H. E. ("Documentary History of Education," by Dr. Hodgins), Vol. I., p. 11.

one hundred boys each, and have a residence for the master, with some rooms for boarders.[11] No steps were taken to carry out these plans until after 1807.

Several private schools were opened prior to 1800. The chief of these were at Newark, York, Ancaster, Cornwall, Kingston, Adolphustown, St. Catharines, and Belleville. Some were evening schools. All were supported by fees. Many were taught by clergymen. The principal subjects were reading, writing, and arithmetic.

On December 17th, 1802, Dr. Baldwin, of York, the father of Hon. Robt. Baldwin, issued the following notice;—[12]

> "Understanding that some of the Gentlemen of this Town have expressed much anxiety for the establishment of a Classical School, Dr. Baldwin begs leave to inform them and the Public that he intends, on Monday, the third day of January next, to open a school, in which he will instruct twelve boys in Reading, Writing, the Classics, and Arithmetic.
>
> "The terms are for each boy, Eight Guineas per annum, to be paid quarterly. One guinea entrance and one cord of wood to be supplied by each boy."

John Strachan, afterwards Bishop Strachan, opened a private school at Kingston in 1799. Later he opened one at Cornwall, and still later one at York. Attempts to open a public school in each District were defeated in the Legislature in 1804 and 1805. In 1806 the sum of £400[13] was appropriated to purchase scientific apparatus.

In 1807, the Legislature took steps to carry out the plan proposed in 1797. There were by this time eight Districts in Upper Canada—Eastern, Johnstown, Midland, Newcastle, Home, Niagara, London, and Western. The sum of £800 was fixed as an annual appropriation to support "a Public School in each and every District in the Province." This meant £100 for each school or teacher. The Legislature also fixed the places where the schools were to be held. The Lieutenant-Governor-in-Council was to appoint not less than five trustees[14] for each District school. These trustees were given almost absolute control over the management of the schools.

It must not be supposed that these schools were public schools in the sense we now attach to that term. Their founders had in mind the great English public school, whose curriculum was largely classical and whose benefits were confined to the wealthy. These schools were not in any sense popular schools. It would seem that Governor Simcoe's proposal in 1798 was to have "Free Grammar Schools."[15] But those established by the Act of 1807 levied considerable sums in fees. They

[11] See D. H. E., Vol. I., p. 21.

[12] See D. H. E., Vol. I., p. 33.

[13] This £400 worth of apparatus was promptly handed over to Mr. Strachan by the Lieutenant-Governor. Mr. Strachan at this time had a private school at Cornwall. It seems quite evident that the apparatus was purchased purposely for his school and at his suggestion. See D. H. E., Vol. I., p. 155.

[14] See D. H. E., Vol. I., p. 61.

[15] See D. H. E., Vol. I., p. 20.

were designed to educate the sons of gentlemen. They were to prepare for professional life. They were essentially for the benefit of the ruling classes. They were largely controlled by Anglicans,[16] and in many cases the teachers were Anglican clergymen.

If these schools were not public schools as we now use the term "public school," neither were they high schools as we now use that term. The curricula had no uniformity. Each school was a law unto itself and depended almost wholly upon the teacher. If he were scholarly and earnest the school would accomplish much. Often very young boys who could scarcely read were admitted. In some schools a fine training in classics was given; in others even the elements of a common education were neglected.

But although these schools were not for the mass of the people, their establishment was none the less an event of far-reaching importance. It was a decided advantage to the mass of the people that their rulers should have some educational advantages. No one can read the lists of names of men educated in these schools and afterwards prominent in Canadian public life without recognizing that their establishment was a blessing to the whole of Canada. They were caste schools, but they kept alive the torch of learning and civilization. Being founded out of public funds, there was created an interest in their welfare among the members of the Legislative Assembly. As years went on and the members of the Assembly came to really represent the people of Upper Canada, they were led to extend to all of the people such educational advantages as had been granted to a section of the people in 1807.

Several efforts were made to repeal the Act of 1807 and substitute for it one of a more popular nature. These efforts were baffled either by the Legislative Council or through the influence of that body in the Assembly itself. A petition[17] presented by sixty-five residents of the Midland District to the Legislature of 1812 will give a fair idea of the state of feeling throughout Upper Canada in regard to education: "Your petitioners . . . feel themselves in duty bound to state that 'An Act to establish Public Schools in each and every District of this Province' is found by experience not to answer the end for which it was designed. Its object, it is presumed, was to promote the education of our youth in general, but a little acquaintance with the facts must convince every unbiased mind that it has contributed little or nothing to the promotion of so laudable a design. By reason of the place of instruction being established at one end of the District, and the sum demanded for tuition, in addition to the annual compensation received from the public, most of the people are unable to avail themselves of the advantages contemplated by the institution. A few wealthy inhabitants, and those of the Town of Kingston, reap exclusively the benefit of it in this District. The institution, instead of aiding the middling and poorer class of His Majesty's subjects, casts money into the lap of the rich, who are sufficiently able, without public assistance, to support a school in every respect

[16] In 1830, when the United Presbytery of Upper Canada petitioned the Legislature against appointing so many Anglicans as trustees of grammar schools, the only reply was that Anglicans had not always been appointed.

[17] See Journals of Legislature of Upper Canada for 1812.

equal to the one established by law. . . . Wherefore, your petitioners pray, that so much of the Act first mentioned may be repealed, and such provisions made in the premises as may be conducive to public utility."

A repeal bill of the Act of 1807 was passed by the Legislative Assembly of 1812, but thrown out by the Legislative Council. The Act of 1807 limited the schools to one for each District. This was unsatisfactory even to that class for whom the schools were especially designed. As the country made progress and became more thickly populated, eight schools were a wholly inadequate provision for the education of those requiring it. But the Legislative Assembly steadily resisted any attempt to enlarge the scope of these class schools. Perhaps it was owing to their resistance that in 1816 they secured the consent of the Legislative Council to a really forward movement in elementary education.

But it would be a serious mistake to infer that the educational machinery of Upper Canada previous to 1816 was limited to these eight District Grammar Schools. What the Government failed to provide, private enterprise secured. More than two hundred schools were certainly in operation in 1816. These schools were maintained partly by subscriptions from well-to-do people and partly by fees collected from the pupils. In many cases they were private ventures, conducted by teachers who depended wholly upon fees. In some cases these schools were of a high order, perhaps superior to the District Grammar Schools; in other cases, probably in the large majority of cases, they were very inefficient. The average fees paid by pupils in the elementary schools were about twelve shillings per quarter.

William Crooks, of Grimsby, writing to Gourlay, in January, 1818, says:[18] "The state of education is also at a very low ebb, not only in this township but generally throughout the District; although the liberality of the Legislature has been great in support of the District Grammar Schools (giving to the teachers of each £100 per annum) yet they have been productive of little or no good hitherto, for this obvious cause, they are looked upon as seminaries exclusively instituted for the education of the children of the more wealthy classes of society, and to which the poor man's child is considered as unfit to be admitted. From such causes, instead of their being a benefit to the Province, they are sunk into obscurity, and the heads of most of them are at this moment enjoying their situations as comfortable sinecures. Another class of schools has within a short time been likewise founded upon the liberality of the Legislative purse denominated as Common or Parish Schools, but like the preceding, the anxiety of the teacher employed seems more alive to his stipend than the advancement of the education of those placed under his care; from the pecuniary advantages thus held out we have been inundated with the worthless scum, under the character of schoolmasters, not only of this but of every other country where the knowledge has been promulgated of the easy means our laws afford of getting a living here, by obtaining a parish school."

The Common or Parish Schools referred to in this letter were the result of the legislation of 1816, a red-letter year in school affairs because it saw the first attempts in Upper Canada to give schools under public control to the common

[18] See Gourlay's "Statistical Account of Upper Canada." Pages 433-434 of Vol. I. Published by Simpkin & Marshall, London, Eng., 1822.

people. The sum of $24,000 a year was appropriated for four years to establish Common Schools. The law provided that the people of any village, town or township might meet together and arrange to establish one or more schools, at each of which the attendance must be not less than twenty. Three suitable trustees were to be chosen to conduct the school, appoint teachers, and select textbooks from a list prescribed by a District Board of Education. The Legislature authorized payments to each of these schools of a sum not exceeding £100. The balance needed to maintain the school had to be made up by subscriptions.

In 1819 the Grammar School Act of 1807 received some slight amendments. The grant of £100 per school was reduced to £50 for new schools, except where the number of pupils exceeded ten. A new school was authorized for the new Gore District, at Hamilton. Trustee Boards were required to present annual reports to the Lieutenant-Governor and to conduct an annual public examination. But the most important change was provision for the free education of ten poor children at each District Public School. These children were chosen by lot from names submitted by Trustee Boards of Common Schools.

In 1822 the Governor, Sir Peregrine Maitland, on his own responsibility, had established in Toronto a school known as the Upper Canada Central School, formed on the plan of the British National Schools, which had been established in Britain by Rev. Dr. Bell. These schools were decidedly Anglican in tone, and that established in Toronto was at the instigation of Rev. Dr. Strachan.[19] In a despatch to Earl Bathurst, Colonial Secretary in 1822, Governor Maitland said:[20] "It is proposed to establish one introductory school on the national plan in each town of a certain size. It is supposed that a salary of £100 per annum to the master of each such school would be sufficient. The number of these schools may be increased as the circumstances of the Province may require and the means allow."

In answer, the Earl of Bathurst, under date of October 12th, 1823, says:[21] "I am happy to have it in my power to convey to you His Majesty's consent that you appropriate a portion of the Reserves set apart for the establishment of a University for the support of schools on the National [Church of England] plan of education." This action established one school, and had in contemplation the establishment of others under the direct control of the Governor and his Council. The Legislative Assembly naturally resented the action, and for two reasons. They objected to the disposal of any Crown property other than upon their authority. They objected to anything being done that would lessen the resources of the proposed University.

A side-light upon education in Upper Canada is furnished by Mr. E. A. Talbot, who published a series of letters upon Upper Canada in London, 1824. I quote from Letter XXX: "The great mass of the [Canadian] people are at present completely ignorant even of the rudiments of the most common learning. Very few can either read or write; and parents who are ignorant themselves, possess so slight a relish for literature and are so little acquainted with its advantages, that they feel scarcely any anxiety to have the minds of their children cultivated. . . . They will

[19] See D. H. E., Vol. I., p. 176.

[20] See copy of despatch in D. H. E., Vol. I., p. 179.

[21] See copy of despatch in D. H. E., Vol. I., p. 179.

not believe that 'knowledge is power,' and being convinced that it is not in the nature of 'book-learned skill' to improve the earnestness of their sons in hewing wood or the readiness of their daughters in spinning flax, they consider it a misapplication of money to spend any sum in obtaining instruction for their offspring. Nothing can afford a stronger proof of their indifference in this respect than the circumstance of their electing men to represent them in the Provincial Parliament, whose attainments in learning are in many instances exceedingly small, and sometimes do not pass beyond the horn-book. I have myself been present in the Honourable the House of Assembly when some of the members, on being called to be Chairmen of Committees, were under the disagreeable and humiliating necessity of requesting other members to read the bills before the Committee, and then, as the different clauses were rejected or adopted, to request these, their proxies, to signify the same in the common mode of writing."

In 1823 there was established a General Board of Education, consisting of: The Hon. and Rev. John Strachan, D.D., Chairman; Hon. Jos. Wells, M.L.C.; Hon. G. H. Markland, M.L.C.; Rev. Robert Addison; John Beverley Robinson, Esq., Attorney-General; Thomas Ridout, Esq., Surveyor-General. The same session of the Legislature set apart £150 as an annual grant for purchasing books and tracts designed to afford moral and religious instruction.

By the creation of a General Board of Education, Rev. Dr. Strachan became very prominently identified with education in Upper Canada. No man was better qualified through zeal, practical knowledge, and a genuine interest in higher education. He had been made an honorary member of the Executive Council in 1815, and an active member in 1817. In 1820 he was appointed a member of the Legislative Council. Being a prominent Churchman, an experienced and successful teacher, and residing at York, he was naturally consulted by successive Governors on educational matters. Strachan was an uncompromising Churchman with ritualistic tendencies, and in politics a Tory of the George III. school. He had neither faith in, nor sympathy for, a democracy. He accepted things as he found them, and wished to preserve them so. He could conceive of no more perfect state of society for the new world than that which he left behind him in the old. He firmly believed in education of the most noble kind for gentlemen, but it is doubtful if he recognized the right of every man to the highest possible cultivation of his intellectual powers. He would have looked upon such a plan as subversive of the existing orders of society. At any rate he never evinced any passion for popular education except that moral and religious education given under the ægis of an Established Church. On the other hand, no man in Canada had a more sincere desire to foster higher institutions of learning, and it had from the very first been Strachan's plan that the District Grammar Schools should be feeders for a Provincial University, and now, in 1824, when he became virtually head of educational affairs in Upper Canada, he determined to carry his scheme to a successful issue.

There were serious difficulties. An endowment had been provided for a university by the Crown grant in 1797, but it was at this time almost worthless. It consisted of blocks of land, containing several townships, in remote parts of the Province. The lands were good, but so long as the Government had free lands to give incoming settlers, the school lands were not in demand. Besides these school or university lands, there were other lands in possession of the Crown. The original surveyor reserved two-sevenths of all land. One-seventh was the reserve for a "Protestant Clergy," which eventually caused so much strife and ill-feeling. The other seventh was known as the Crown Reserve. In many cases this Crown Reserve was becoming valuable, even in 1824, because of the labour of settlers who owned adjoining farms. Much of the Crown Reserve was under lease and giving a more or less certain revenue. Strachan conceived a bold and successful plan. He suggested to Sir Peregrine Maitland that for grants to new settlers the school lands were worth as much to the Government as the Crown Reserves. Why not exchange school lands for an equal area of Crown Reserve land? The matter was put before the Home Government, and in 1827 a favourable reply was given. The result was that the University got 225,944 acres of land, distributed throughout every District in Upper Canada, but having more than one-half its total area in the Home, Gore, and London Districts, the wealthiest and most populous parts of Upper Canada. The Commissioners, appointed in 1848 by Lord Elgin to enquire into the affairs of King's College, state (pages 16 and 17): "The Crown Reserves thus converted into the University Endowment, consisted of lands in various parts of Upper Canada in actual or nominal occupation under lease, at rate of rental fixed by a certain scale established by the Provincial Government, and a large proportion of the lots were in an improved or cultivated state."

In March, 1826, Rev. Dr. Strachan submitted to the Lieutenant-Governor a very able and comprehensive report[22] showing why a university ought at once to be established. The report gives an interesting and authentic summary of the state of education in Upper Canada at that time. "The present state of Education in this Province consists of Common Schools throughout the Townships, established under several Acts of the Provincial Legislature, and which are now, by the exertions of Your Excellency, placed on an excellent footing, requiring no other improvements than the means of multiplying their number, which, no doubt, will be granted as the finances of the Province become more productive. In about three hundred and forty Common Schools established in the different Districts of the Colony, from seven to eight thousand children are taught reading and writing, the elements of arithmetic, and the first principles of religion; and when it is considered that the parents commonly send their children in rotation—the younger in summer when the roads are good, and the older in winter—it is not too much to say that nearly double this number, or from twelve to fourteen thousand children, profit annually by the Common Schools. The consequence is that the people, scattered as they are over a vast wilderness, are becoming alive to the great advantage of educating their children, and are, in many places, seconding, with laudable zeal, the exertions of the Legislature, and establishing schools at their own expense.

"Provision is made by law for the translation of some of the more promising scholars from the Common to the District Schools, where the classics and practical mathematics are taught. In these schools, eleven in number, there are at present upwards of 300 youth acquiring an education to qualify them for the different

[22] See copy in D. H. E., Vol. I., pp. 211-213.

professions; and, although they can seldom support more than one master, several of the young gentlemen who have been brought up in them are now eminent in their professions, and would, by their talents and high principles, do credit to seminaries of greater name. But the period has arrived when the District Schools [Grammar Schools] will become still more useful by confining themselves to the intention of their first establishment, namely, nurseries for a University—an institution now called for by the increased population and circumstances of the Colony, and most earnestly desired by the more respectable inhabitants.

"There is not in either Province any English Seminary above the rank of a good school, at which a liberal education can be obtained. Thus the youth of nearly 300,000 Englishmen have no opportunity of receiving instruction within the Canadas in Law, Medicine, or Divinity. The consequence is that many young men coming forward to the learned professions are obliged to look beyond the Province for the last two years of their education—undoubtedly the most important and critical of their lives. Very few are able on account of the great expense to go to England or Scotland; and the distance is so great and the difficulties so many that parental anxiety reluctantly trusts children from its observation and control. The youths are, therefore, in some degree, compelled to look forward to the United States, where the means of education, though of a description far inferior to those of Great Britain, are yet superior to those within the Province, and a growing necessity is arising of sending them to finish their education in that country. Now, in the United States, a system prevails unknown to, or unpractised by, any other nation. In all other countries morals and religion are made the basis of future instruction, and the first book put into the hands of children teaches them the domestic, social, and religious virtues; but in the United States politics pervade the whole system of instruction. The school books from the very first elements are stuffed with praises of their own institutions and breathe hatred to everything English. To such a country our youth may go, strongly attached to their native land and all its establishments, but by hearing them continually depreciated and those of America praised, these attachments will, in many, be gradually weakened, and some may become fascinated with that liberty which has degenerated into licentiousness and imbibe, perhaps unconsciously, sentiments unfriendly to things of which Englishmen are proud. . . .

"The establishment of a University at the seat of Government will complete a regular system of education in Upper Canada from the letters of the alphabet to the most profound investigations of science. . . . In regard to the profession of medicine it is melancholy to think that more than three-fourths of the present practitioners have been educated or attended lectures in the United States. . . . There are, as yet, only twenty-two clergymen in Upper Canada, the greater number from England. It is essential that young men coming forward to the Church should be educated entirely within the Province, but for this there is no provision. . . . But the wants of the Province are becoming great, and however much disposed the elder clergy may be to bring forward young men to the sacred profession, they have neither time nor means of doing it with sufficient effect. There can be nothing of that zeal, of that union and mutual attachment, of that deep theological and literary enquiry and anxiety to excel, which would be found among men collected at the University, and here it is not irrelevant to observe that it is of the greatest importance that the education of the Colony should be conducted by the clergy.

"Nothing can be more manifest than that this Colony has not yet felt the advantage of a religious establishment. What can twenty-two clergymen do, scattered over a country of nearly six hundred miles in length? Can we be surprised that, under such circumstances, the religious benefits of the ecclesiastical establishment are unknown, and sectaries of all descriptions have increased on every side? And when it is further considered that the religious teachers of all other Protestant denominations, a very few respectable ministers of the Church of Scotland excepted, come almost universally from the Republican States of America, where they gather their knowledge and form their sentiments, it is evident that if the Imperial Government does not step forward with efficient help, the mass of the population will be nurtured and instructed in hostility to all our institutions, both civil and religious. . . . From all which it appears highly expedient to establish a university at the seat of Government, to complete the system of education in the Colony at which all the branches requisite for qualifying young men for the learned professions may be taught. . . . The principal and professors, except those of Medicine and Law, should be clergymen of the Established Church; and no tutor, teacher, or officer who is not a member of that Church should ever be employed in the institution."

I have given this long quotation from Rev. Dr. Strachan's report for several reasons. It shows very clearly the point of view of a remarkable man who had much to do with educational affairs in Upper Canada for a period of nearly seventy years. It shows his zeal for higher education, his belief in the efficacy of a religious establishment, his narrow bigotry and intolerance of all outside of an establishment, his old-world belief that the clergy should control education, his loyal attachment to British institutions, and above all, to those who read between the lines, his lack of real interest in elementary education. He is perfectly satisfied with the state of the Common Schools, although they were then accommodating less than one in twenty of the total population. The schools of which he says, "which are now, by the exertions of Your Excellency, placed on an excellent footing, requiring no other improvements than the means of multiplying their number," were conducted in rude buildings, without any apparatus, with a motley assortment of textbooks, and taught in many cases by ignorant itinerant schoolmasters who were of no use at any other occupation, and who received from $80 to $200 a year! Little can ever be expected in the way of improvement from those who are wholly satisfied with present conditions, and it is safe to say that any improvements that took place in the Common Schools of Canada under the *régime* of the Rev. Dr. Strachan were owing to other causes than the efforts put forth by that gentleman. The Common Schools of Upper Canada had to wait for a new birth—until Ryerson breathed life into them.

Rev. Dr. Strachan's Report is interesting for another reason—it deals with the proposed King's College and its relations with what Dr. Strachan calls the "religious establishment" in Canada. This "religious establishment" was to have as its basis the one-seventh of all lands in Upper Canada as provided for by the Constitutional Act of 1791. Now these two things, the Clergy Reserves and King's College, caused more trouble to the Canadian Legislature and engendered more bitter feeling among the people of Upper Canada than any other two questions that ever were debated in the Parliament of Upper Canada, or in the Parliament of the united Canadas. In the Parliamentary struggle over both these questions the Rev. Dr. Strachan was an active and valiant leader of the party of privilege, and among those who led the opposing forces to a final victory none was more courageous or more successful than Dr. Ryerson.

Dr. Strachan went to England in 1826 to use his personal influence towards securing a Royal Charter for a University. He there issued an appeal to the English people for aid on the ground that the proposed College would be largely occupied in educating clergymen for the Anglican Church.[23] A Royal Charter, making the proposed university a close corporation under the control of Anglican clergymen, was obtained. Besides granting the charter the British Government made a grant toward buildings of £1,000 a year for sixteen years.

When the Legislative Assembly met in 1828 several members presented numerously signed petitions praying for definite information about the newly granted charter of King's College. The Governor sent down a copy of the charter which was referred to a select committee. The committee protested against the nature of the charter in that the university was to become an Anglican institution, supported out of public funds. This they thought unjust, inasmuch as only a small proportion of the settlers of Upper Canada were Anglicans.[24] The committee also drafted an address to His Majesty the King. This address was adopted by the Assembly, and immediately despatched to His Majesty by the Governor. The address was courteous and loyal in tone, but the exact condition of affairs in Canada was made clear. The King was petitioned to cancel the charter to King's College, and grant one that would make possible a university for all classes. This address to His Majesty and the protest of the Assembly of Upper Canada attracted the attention of a select committee of the Imperial Parliament. This committee[25] reported against that part of the Charter which required religious tests. George Ryerson, of Canada, gave valuable evidence before this committee relative to Canadian affairs. It seems doubtful whether His Majesty's advisers, when the King's College charter was given, were really made aware of the conditions of society in Canada. Those Canadians who had the ears of His Majesty's advisers were, for the most part, interested in forming and strengthening an Anglican Establishment.

[23] See "An Appeal to the Friends of Religion and Literature in behalf of the University of Upper Canada." By John Strachan, Archdeacon of York, Upper Canada, 1826.

[24] See Journals of House of Assembly for Upper Canada, 1828.

[25] See Report made 22nd July, 1828, by Select Committee of House of Commons, appointed to inquire into the State of Civil Government in Canada.

CHAPTER III.

EDUCATION IN UPPER CANADA FROM 1783 TO 1844—(CONTINUED).

Late in the year 1828, Sir Peregrine Maitland was replaced as Lieutenant-Governor of Upper Canada by Sir John Colborne. About the same time Sir George Murray, who had acted as Administrator of the Government of Upper Canada in 1815, and who consequently knew something of Canadian affairs, became Colonial Secretary in the Imperial Parliament. In acknowledging receipt of the petition to His Majesty of the Assembly of Upper Canada protesting against the King's College charter, Sir George Murray, in a communication to Sir John Colborne, said:[26] "It would be deservedly a subject of regret to His Majesty's Government, if the University, recently established at York, should prove to have been founded upon principles which cannot be made to accord with the general feelings and opinions of those for whose advantage it was intended. . . . I have observed that your predecessor (Sir Peregrine Maitland) in the Government of Upper Canada differs from the House of Assembly as to the general prevalence of objections to the University founded upon the degree of exclusive connection which it has with the Church of England. It seems reasonable to conclude, however, that on such a subject as this an address adopted by a full House of Assembly, with scarcely any dissentient voices,[27] must be considered to express the prevailing opinion in the Province upon this subject.

"In the event, therefore, of its appearing to you to be proper to invite the Legislative Council and House of Assembly to resume the consideration of this question, you will apprise them that their representations on the existing charter of the University have attracted the serious attention of His Majesty's Government and that the opinion which may be expressed by the Legislative Council and House of Assembly on that subject will not fail to receive the most prompt and serious attention."

Shortly after the receipt of this communication Sir John Colborne, as Chancellor of King's College, convened the College Council and declared that no immediate steps were to be taken toward active University work, and that not one stone should be put upon another until certain alterations had been made in the charter.

In 1829 the Chairman of the General Board of Education, Rev. Dr. Strachan, presented to the Legislative Assembly his first annual report. It is an able and very

[26] See copy of Sir George Murray's letter in D. H. E., Vol. I., pp. 257 and 258.

[27] The vote stood 21 for and 9 against.

suggestive document. It showed 372 pupils[28] in the eleven Grammar Schools, and 401 Common Schools with 10,712 pupils. Dr. Strachan had personally visited each Grammar School during 1828, and had incidentally learned something of the Common Schools. Referring to Grammar Schools he says:[29] "It will be seen that in some places girls are admitted.[30] This happens from the want of good female schools, and perhaps from the more rapid progress which children are supposed to make under experienced and able schoolmasters. It is to be wished, however, that separate schools for the sexes were established, as the admission of female children interferes with the government which is required in classical seminaries; it is, nevertheless, an inconvenience of a temporary nature, which will gradually pass away as the population increases in wealth and numbers." This "inconvenience of a temporary nature" persisted until 1868, when girls were formally admitted as pupils in Grammar Schools.

Dr. Strachan pointed out very clearly in this Report that the Common Schools could never improve very much until the teachers were better paid. He also made an excellent practical suggestion.[31] "The Provincial Board, therefore, would submit with all deference, that in addition to the public allowance, even if increased beyond its present amount, a power should be given to the Townships to assess themselves for this special purpose."

Here we have laid down the correct principle of support for public schools, and one cannot but feel that had Dr. Strachan followed up this suggestion by pressing it upon the Legislature, and by discussing it with school-managers and the general public, he might have secured its early adoption.

When the Legislature convened in 1829, Sir John Colborne in the Speech from the Throne[32] made direct reference to education as follows: "The Public [Grammar] Schools are generally increasing, but their organization appears susceptible of improvement. Measures will be adopted, I hope, to reform the Royal Grammar School [the District School at York] and to incorporate it with the University recently endowed by His Majesty, and to introduce a system in that Seminary which will open to the youth of the Province the means of receiving a liberal and extensive course of instruction. Unceasing exertions should be made to attract able masters to this country, where the population bears no proportion to the number of offices and employments that must necessarily be held by men of education and acquirements, for the support of the laws and of your free institutions."

This message from the Governor may require some explanation. In the first place let us note that Sir John Colborne was an able and enlightened man, sincerely desirous of giving to Upper Canada a government that would be acceptable to the mass of the people. He seems to have realized clearly that the Assembly was a fairly accurate reflection of public opinion, and that no policy could ulti-

[28] In 1827 there were 329 pupils, of whom 8 in the Cornwall School were girls.

[29] See copy of Report in D. H. E., Vol. I., pp. 266 and 267.

[30] The Report for 1828 showed 25 girls in the eleven District Schools.

[31] See original Report in Appendix to Journals of Assembly, U. C., pp. 16 and 17 of Appendix on Education.

[32] See Journals of Assembly for U. C. for 1829, p. 5.

mately prevail unless it was in harmony with its wishes. His action in arresting the working of King's College was one proof of this, although his subsequent action in founding Upper Canada College solely on his own responsibility showed his belief in the power of the Crown to take independent action. He saw that the District Grammar Schools were very inefficient and were touching the lives of an insignificant proportion of the people of Upper Canada. He foresaw that for some years the revenue to be derived from the endowment of King's College would not support a very pretentious institution, and that for such an institution, even if it were in operation, there would be very few students prepared by previous study to profit from its courses. In his opinion the immediate wants of the country would be better served by a high-class school than by a university. Hence his proposal to reform the Royal Grammar School at York and incorporate it with King's College.

The Assembly of 1829 contained many eminent men, of whom it is sufficient to mention Marshall Bidwell (the Speaker), William Lyon Mackenzie, W. W. Baldwin (father of Hon. Robert Baldwin), and John Rolph, the latter a graduate of the University of Cambridge. The Assembly appointed a select committee on Education. This committee made an extensive report[33] upon both District Grammar and Common Schools. In regard to the former they were pronounced in their condemnation and recommended their abolition. The report claimed that the District or Grammar School Trustees, appointed by the Crown, were chosen to promote the interests of the Anglican Church; that in many cases the schools themselves were merely stepping-stones for the clergy of the Anglican Church; that they were under no efficient inspection; that they were quite as expensive to those parents who did not live immediately beside them as much better schools in the United States; and finally that as only 108 pupils in the whole Province were studying languages in these schools, that their work could be done equally well by really good Common Schools. The report lamented the low salaries of teachers in Common Schools and suggested that no Government grants should be given unless the managers of schools themselves raised by subscription equal amounts. The report also protested against the payment out of public funds of £300 a year to Rev. Dr. Strachan, as Chairman of the General Board,[34] and against his assumption that reports of District Schools should be made to him instead of to the Lieutenant-Governor. The report expressed a hope that something might be done to encourage the publication of textbooks in Canada, and concluded with expressing approval of the Governor's plan to found a seminary of a high class, which should be free from sectarian influences and afford advanced instruction to the youth of Canada.

Later in the session of 1829 this select committee on Education prepared a series of resolutions which were adopted by the Assembly. The following are the chief points in the resolutions:—[35]

1. That the Governor, or Lieutenant-Governor of the Province, not being amenable for his conduct to any tribunal, ought not to be Chancellor of King's

[33] See Report in Appendix to Journals of Assembly for 1829, p. 42.

[34] The General Board of Education had been organized by Sir Peregrine Maitland wholly on his own authority and that of the Home Government. The Assembly naturally refused to acknowledge any obligation to support it with public funds.

[35] See Appendix to Journals of Assembly of U.C. for 1829, pp. 72 and 73.

College.

2. That it ought not to be required that the President of King's College be a clergyman of the Anglican Church, and that he ought to be elected or appointed for a stated term.

3. That the Archdeacon of York ought not by virtue of his clerical office to become President of King's College.

4. That the President and Professors of King's College ought not to be required to subscribe to the Thirty-nine Articles.

5. That the Degree of Doctor of Divinity ought to be conferred by King's College upon any professing Christian who passed the required examinations in Classical, Biblical, and other subjects of learning.

6. That wherever the charter of King's College is in any way sectarian it should be amended.

The Governor asked the Legislative Council to consider in what way the charter of King's College could be amended to make it more acceptable to the people of Upper Canada. The Council in reply recommended that instead of the Archdeacon of York any Anglican clergyman should be eligible for President. They also recommended that tests for the Council be dispensed with.

Having the sanction of the Home Government, and feeling sure of the active support of the Assembly, Sir John Colborne immediately put in execution his plan of forming a high-class school to replace the Royal Grammar School at York. He caused advertisements to be inserted in the British papers for masters. The head master was to have a house, £600 per annum, and the privilege of taking boarders. The classical and mathematical masters were to receive £300 a year and similar privileges. The Assembly had suggested that the new school should be known as Colborne College, but the name adopted was Upper Canada College. The school opened in 1830 with a staff of seven specialists, nearly all chosen in England. The work was carried on in the buildings of the old Grammar School until handsome and elaborate buildings were erected on Russell Square, north of King Street. An endowment of some 60,000 acres from the School lands was given the new institution. It was generally felt that the new school would, for the present, supply the want of a university, and also make it unnecessary for Canadian youths to complete their education in the United States.

Before Upper Canada College had been working a year a very numerously-signed petition was presented by some York patrons of the school praying for some modification of the exclusively classical nature of the programme for those boys destined for commerce and mechanical pursuits. The Governor's attempt to give Canadians a high-class collegiate school seemed only partially successful. The error was in attempting to adapt to a new country a form of school that suited the requirements of a select class in an old and highly civilized country. Latin and Greek must be crammed into boys whether or not they had any natural aptitude for language study, and quite irrespective of their future occupations in life.

The founding and liberal equipment of Upper Canada College had one effect that might easily have been foretold. Petitions came from almost every Grammar School District praying for endowed and well-equipped schools similar to Upper Canada College. The petitioners resented the concentration at York of two important institutions, Upper Canada College and King's College, deriving support from an endowment originally set aside to give educational facilities to the whole of Upper Canada.

The Assembly of 1833, through a select committee, made a minute examination into the affairs of Upper Canada College, and passed a resolution recommending that it be incorporated with King's College. I give here quotations from two writers on Upper Canada College, showing how differently things appear when viewed through different eyes. The first is from a letter written in 1833 by Rev. Thomas Radcliffe.[36] "Future generations will bless the memory of Sir John Colborne, who, to the many advantages derived from the equity and wisdom of his government, has added that of a magnificent foundation [in Upper Canada College] for the purposes of literary instruction. The lowest salary of any of the professors of this institution is £300 per annum, with the accommodation of a noble brick house and the privilege of taking boarders at £50 per annum."

The next is from "Sketches," published by William Lyon Mackenzie, London, 1833. "Splendid incomes are given to the masters of the new [Upper Canada] College, culled at Oxford by the Vice-Chancellor, and dwellings furnished to the professors (we may say) by the sweat of the brow of the Canadian labourer. All these advantages and others not now necessary to be mentioned, are insufficient to gratify the rapacious appetite of the 'Established Church' managers, who, in order to accumulate wealth and live in opulence, charge the children of His Majesty's subjects ten times as high fees as are required by the less amply endowed Seminary at Quebec. They have another reason for so doing. The College (already a monopoly) becomes almost an exclusive school for the families of the Government officers, and the few who, through their means, have, in York, already attained a pecuniary independence out of the public treasury. The College never was intended for the people, nor did the Executive endow it thus amply that all classes might apply to the fountain of knowledge."[37]

As time passed the College founded by Sir John Colborne did good work as a secondary school for people of wealth, but all attempts to make it popular with the mass of the people proved ineffective. The Legislature gave it an annual grant somewhat unwillingly.[38] The buildings were erected, and part of the annual expenses paid from advances made by the King's College Council.

By an Act passed in 1839[39] there was an attempt made to raise the College to the dignity of a temporary university. This action displeased the Council of King's College because it tended to delay the opening of lectures in that institution. In 1849, when the Baldwin University Bill made an independent corporation of Upper Canada College, that institution was indebted to the University for near-

[36] See copy of letter in D. H. E., Vol. II., pp. 120 and 121.
[37] See volume in Library of Parliament, Ottawa, pp. 190 and 191.
[38] See D. H. E., Vol. III., p. 123.
[39] See D. H. E., Vol. III., pp. 170 and 171.

ly $40,000, which was never repaid.[40]

In 1831 the Methodists began to build at Cobourg the Upper Canada Academy, which was to be open to all religious denominations. They felt that although Upper Canada College was non-sectarian in a legal sense, yet, inasmuch as the principal and professors were Anglican clergymen, the institution was essentially an Anglican College.

At this time the Rev. Egerton Ryerson was editor of *The Christian Guardian* newspaper, the official organ of the Methodist Conference. In an editorial, April, 1831, he thus refers to the proposed Upper Canada Academy: "It is the first literary institution which has been commenced by any body of ministers in accordance with the frequently expressed wishes of the people of Upper Canada. The Methodist Conference have not sought endowments of public lands for the establishment of an institution, contrary to the voice of the people as expressed by their representatives. . . . Desirous of promoting more extensively the interests of the rising generation and of the country generally, we have resolved upon the establishment of a Seminary of Learning—we have done so upon liberal principles—we have not reserved any peculiar privileges to ourselves for the education of our children; we have published the constitution for your examination; and now we appeal to your liberality for assistance. . . . On the characteristics of the system of education which it is contemplated to pursue in the proposed Seminary, we may observe that it will be such as to produce habits of intellectual labour and activity; a diligent and profitable improvement of time; bodily health and vigour, a fitness and relish for agricultural and mechanical, as well as for other pursuits; virtuous principles and Christian morals. On the importance of education generally we may remark, it is as necessary as the light—it should be as common as water, and as free as air. . . . Education among the people is the best security of a good government and constitutional liberty; it yields a steady, unbending support to the former, and effectually protects the latter. An educated people are always a loyal people to good government; and the first object of a wise government should be the education of the people. An educated people are always enterprising in all kinds of general and local improvements. An ignorant population are equally fit for, and are liable to be, slaves of despots and the dupes of demagogues; sometimes, like the unsettled ocean, they can be thrown into incontrollable agitation by every wind that blows; at other times, like the uncomplaining ass, they tamely submit to the most unreasonable burdens. . . . Sound learning is of great worth even in religion; the wisest and best instructed Christians are the most steady, and may be the most useful. If a man be a child in knowledge he is likely to be tossed to and fro, and carried about with every wind of doctrine, and often lies at the mercy of interested, designing men; the more knowledge he has the safer is his state. If our circumstances be such that we have few means of improvement, we should turn them to the best account. Partial knowledge is better than total ignorance; and he who cannot get all he may wish, must take heed to acquire all that he can. If total ignorance be a bad and dangerous thing, every degree of knowledge lessens both the evil and the danger."[41]

[40] For the later history of Upper Canada College see "History of Upper Canada College," by Principal George Dickson.

[41] See copy of letter in D. H. E., Vol. II., pp. 7 and 8.

Ryerson wrote this when he was only twenty-eight years of age, but it foreshadows the fundamental principles upon which he later attempted to base a national system of education.

It is interesting to note that in this same year the United Presbytery of Upper Canada were discussing the establishment of a Literary and Theological Seminary at Pleasant Bay, in Prince Edward County. This seminary never was established, but the agitation for it led to the founding of Queen's University, at Kingston.

While Methodist and Presbyterian clergy were forming plans for academies, the members of the Legislative Assembly were debating a series of resolutions on the School Reserves and the failure of the people of Upper Canada to secure the free Grammar Schools for which the Crown Lands were appropriated in 1798. Several things are made plain in these resolutions regarding the attitude of the popularly elected branch of the Legislature. The following stand out prominently:—

1. That the existing Grammar Schools were wholly inadequate to perform the work for which they were created.

2. That the real intentions of the Crown in setting apart the immense School Reserves in 1798 had never been carried out.

3. That the successive Canadian Administrations had been largely concerned in appropriating the lion's share of these Reserves for University education.

4. That the School Reserves of 1798, with proper management, would be now (1831) sufficiently productive to give great assistance to education if applied in accord with the real wishes of the people.

5. That the money received from these School lands from time to time ought to be paid in to the Receiver-General and disposed of only by vote of the Legislature.

Further protests were made against the exclusive nature of King's College charter, and the Assembly was assured by Sir John Colborne that some changes would be made. As a matter of fact, on the 2nd of November, 1831, Lord Goderich, the British Colonial Secretary, in a lengthy communication to Governor Colborne, showed that His Majesty's Government was fully seized of the situation in regard to the charter of King's College. Lord Goderich said,[42] "I am to convey through you to the Members of the Corporation of King's College, at the earnest recommendation and advice of His Majesty's Government, that they do forthwith surrender[43] to His Majesty the charter of King's College of Upper Canada, with any lands that may have been granted them." Lord Goderich then proceeds to intimate that a new charter will be granted by the Legislature of Upper Canada. Lord Goderich further proceeds to give some very sound advice concerning the necessity of mutual forbearance among a people of diverse religious creeds.

In the Assembly there was shown an intelligent grasp of the educational needs of the country and a determination to secure better schools. Had the Executive Council and Legislative Council been equally zealous in the cause of education, the fathers and mothers of the generation which profited from Ryerson's reforms

[42] See copy of despatch in D. H. E., Vol. II., p. 55.

[43] This the College Council positively refused to do.

might themselves have had the advantage of good schools.

The following extracts from an address to His Excellency, Sir John Colborne, will show the temper and wishes of the Assembly: "We, His Majesty's dutiful and loyal subjects, the Commons of Upper Canada in Provincial Parliament assembled, most respectfully beg leave to represent that there is in this Province a very general want of education; that the insufficiency of the Common School fund [the total Government grant for schools in 1831 was $11,200] to support competent, respectable, and well-educated teachers, has degraded Common School teaching from a regular business to a mere matter of convenience to transient persons, or common idlers, who often teach the school one season and leave it vacant until it accommodates some other like person to take it in hand, whereby the minds of our youth are left without cultivation, or, what is still worse, frequently with vulgar, low-bred, vicious, or intemperate examples before them in the capacity of monitors."[44] The address proceeded to state that there was urgent need of a Government fund to secure larger grants for teachers' salaries, and asked His Excellency to lay before the Colonial Secretary a plan to set aside one million acres of waste land in Upper Canada for the support of Common Schools.

In this Address the Assembly virtually said to the Crown, "Give us some fixed capital as a source of revenue and we will speedily reorganize our schools." The Assembly knew what was needed and knew how to remedy the existing conditions, but was powerless because the Crown revenue was subject only to the control of the Executive Council.

The session of 1832-33[45] was very active from an educational point of view. The Assembly was informed by His Excellency that the Crown had consented to give over to the Legislature, for the support of Grammar Schools, control of the 258,330 acres of School lands, being the balance of the original grant of half a million acres made in 1798, and from which had already been made extensive grants to endow King's College and Upper Canada College. Much of the remainder of this land, which was now vested in the Legislature, was not of a superior quality. It had also been selected in township blocks and naturally had very little value until settlements were made in surrounding townships.

The Assembly prepared an Address to His Majesty praying for a grant of one million acres of Crown lands for the establishment and support of Township Common Schools. As a measure of immediate relief for these schools, a bill was passed by the two branches of the Legislature, and assented to by His Excellency, providing for two years an additional grant of $22,000. This sum was allotted to the several Districts, approximately in proportion to population, but no Board of Trustees was to receive any of this grant unless they secured for their teacher a sum equal at least to twice the Government grant.

The most significant feature of the session, however, was a Common School

[44] See Journals of Assembly, U. C., 1831, p. 40.

[45] The previous session, William Lyon Mackenzie had been expelled from the Assembly because of his criticism of the Governor, in his newspaper, the *Colonial Advocate*. It is interesting to note that Mackenzie's criticisms of the Governor were largely based on His Excellency's actions in regard to education.

Bill, introduced into the Assembly by Mr. Mahlon Burwell, and read a first time. The bill proposed to repeal all previous Common School legislation; to establish a General Board and also District Boards of Education; to grant £10,000 to Common Schools as a Legislative grant and to assess a further £10,000 on the rateable property of the Districts.

This bill, had it become law, would have anticipated Ryerson's legislation by nearly twenty years, and it is interesting to note the comments made upon it by that gentleman, who was at this time editor of the *Christian Guardian*. The *Guardian* of January 15th, 1834, expressed a general approval of the plan of taxation but was totally opposed to the *appointment* of Boards of Education. After showing that the principle of local taxation was borrowed from the New England States, where it was working satisfactorily, Ryerson says: "The next leading feature of the bill is the appointment of a General Board of Education and also District Boards of Education. This is proposed to be left to the Governor, or person administering the Government, a proposition, in our opinion, radically objectionable. It makes the system of education, in theory, a mere engine of the Executive, a system which is liable to all the abuse, suspicion, jealousy and opposition caused by despotism; and it withholds from the system of Common School education, in its first and prominent feature, that character of common interest and harmonious co-operation which, as we humbly conceive, are essential to its success, and even to its acceptance with the Province. Education is an object in which the Government, as an individual portion of the Province, and the people at large possess, in some respects, a common interest, consequently they should exercise a joint or common control. . . . And in an equitable and patriotic administration of Government, the more its agents and the people's agents are associated together in promoting the common weal, the more strongly will mutual respect and confidence and co-operation between the people and the Government be established, the less room there will be for Executive negligence, or partiality, or popular or local abuse; and the less opportunity there will be for either despotic oppression or demagogue misrepresentation."

In 1834 there was a General Election, which resulted in the return to the Assembly of a large majority in favour of reform principles, and wholly opposed to the arbitrary and aristocratic ideas of the Legislative Council. Bidwell, Rolph, and William Lyon Mackenzie were three leading spirits in the new House.

When the Assembly opened the Governor laid before the members a despatch from the Colonial Office, stating His Majesty's readiness to transfer 240,000 acres in the settled townships in return for the School lands which were in township blocks and not then saleable.

A bill was passed by the Legislature renewing for two years, 1835 and 1836, the increased grant of £5,650 for Common Schools.

A grant of £200 was also made to Mechanics' Institutes at York and a grant of £100 to one at Kingston.

Considerable time was spent in the Assembly upon two bills which were rejected by the Executive Council. One was a bill to regulate Common Schools which would have given them a thorough organization and made them subject to popular control by elected Boards and Superintendents. The Executive Council had no faith in control by the people. They doubted whether "the respectable yeomanry of the country" were capable of choosing suitable Superintendents. The other was a bill to amend the charter of King's College. These amendments were designed to remove all religious tests and to have the College governed by a Council, half of whom were to be appointed by the Assembly and half by the Legislative Council. The only reasons given by the Council for rejecting these amendments were that they knew of no university so governed and that a university must have as a basis some established form of religion. In the meantime, while the hide-bound worshippers of European traditions who made up the Council were delaying the active work of King's College, the youth of Upper Canada, preparing for the learned professions, were compelled to seek university advantages in the United States or Great Britain. More than this, owing to the lack of advantages in their own country, many who could otherwise have afforded it were wholly deprived of the higher education and training necessary for the professions they had in view.

The Legislative Council at this time, and for many years afterwards, made boasts of their loyalty to the Crown, and upon some occasions arrogated to themselves and their friends a monopoly of all loyal spirit in Upper Canada, and yet they firmly refused to surrender the charter and endowment of King's College when requested and even urged to do so by His Majesty's Colonial Secretary[46]. From 1831 to 1835, the Council refused to accept any substantial amendments made in that charter suggested by the Assembly, although Lord Goderich had, in 1831, made it quite clear that His Majesty's Government wished the question of the charter to be settled by the Upper Canada Legislature.

When, upon the 6th of May, 1835, Sir John Colborne sent to the Colonial Secretary the King's College Charter Amendment Bill passed by the Assembly, he urged the immediate opening of King's College, although he had declared to the College Council that "not one stone should be placed upon another" until the charter was amended. It may also be gathered from this despatch to Lord Glenelg[47] that Sir John Colborne accompanied it with a draft of amendments which he thought would be acceptable to both branches of the Legislature of Upper Canada. His Lordship was too astute a politician and too thoroughly informed concerning Canadian public opinion to be easily misled. Sir John Colborne, as a concession to the Assembly, proposed that five out of seven of the governing body should be permanently of the faith of the Church of England. The other two members were to be the Lieutenant-Governor and the Archdeacon of York! Lord Glenelg, in reply, says: "I cannot hesitate to express my opinion that this plan claims for the Established Church of England privileges which those who best understand and most deeply prize her real interests would not think it prudent to assert for her in any British Province on the North American Continent. . . . I would respectfully and earnestly impress upon the Members of both these Bodies [Assembly and Council] the expediency of endeavouring, by mutual concessions, to meet on some common ground. Especially would I beg the Legislative Councillors to remember

[46] See letter of Lord Goderich of Nov. 2nd, 1831, to Sir John Colborne.

[47] See D. H. E., Vol. II., p. 214.

that, if there be any one subject on which, more than others, it is vain and dangerous to oppose the deliberate wishes of the great mass of the people, the system of national instruction to be pursued in the moral and religious education of youth is emphatically that subject."[48] Lord Glenelg concludes by referring the question of amending the charter back to the Legislature of Upper Canada and states that His Majesty will act as mediator only if the two branches of the Legislature fail to agree and then only upon their presenting a joint Address.

[48] See copy of letter in D. H. E., Vol. II., pp. 213 and 214.

CHAPTER IV.

EDUCATION IN UPPER CANADA FROM 1783 TO 1844—(CONTINUED).

During the Legislative session of 1836, Sir John Colborne was replaced by Sir Francis Bond Head as Lieutenant-Governor. It would seem that the difference of opinion between Sir John Colborne and Lord Glenelg of the Colonial Office was responsible for the former's asking to be recalled. His last official act as Lieutenant-Governor of Upper Canada, and one intimately connected with educational controversy at a later date, was to sign patents for the endowment of forty-three Anglican rectories out of the Clergy Reserve lands.

In the Legislature no real progress was made in education, although a lengthy report[49] and a draft School Bill were presented by a member of the Assembly, Doctor Charles Duncomb. This report was based on a visit paid by Doctor Duncomb to the Eastern, Middle and Western United States. It is interesting and emphasizes the importance of a suitable education for women.

The most important event of the year in its after effects upon education in Upper Canada was the formal opening of Upper Canada Academy[50] at Cobourg, under a Royal Charter secured by Egerton Ryerson.

In resigning his position as editor of *The Guardian*, the official organ of Methodism, Ryerson referred to the condition of education in Upper Canada, emphasizing the supreme importance of elementary instruction for every child in the country. It is also interesting to note that at this date, when he had probably never dreamed of having any official connection with elementary education, he should have touched the very root of the problem by pointing out the utter impossibility of making any real progress without a body of educated and trained teachers.

The Legislature of 1837 set at rest for a few years the vexed question of an amendment to King's College charter. The majority of the Legislative Council were stoutly opposed to any modifications that would lessen the control of the Anglican Church, but they saw that public opinion was strong enough to prevent the opening of the college until amendments were made. They also saw that they were running a risk of having the charter cancelled and a new one granted by the Crown. They accordingly accepted certain amendments proposed by the Legisla-

---

[49] See Appendix to Journals of Assembly of U.C., 1836. See also Assembly Journals for 1836, pp. 213 and 214.

[50] See Chapter I.

tive Assembly. These amendments[51] gave *ex-officio* seats on the College Council to the Speaker of the two branches of the Legislature and to the Attorney-General and the Solicitor-General of Upper Canada; they removed from members of the Council and from professors every semblance of a religious test except the following declaration: "I do solemnly and sincerely declare that I believe in the authenticity and Divine Inspiration of the Old and New Testaments and in the Doctrine of the Holy Trinity"; they removed absolutely from religious tests all students and candidates for degrees; they made the Judges of His Majesty's Court of King's Bench visitors instead of the Lord Bishop of Quebec, and vested the appointment of future presidents in His Majesty instead of conferring that office *ex-officio* upon the Archdeacon of York.

Steps were taken at once to place the college in a position to begin work. A very able and comprehensive scheme[52] of studies and courses was drawn up by the President, Dr. Strachan, and everything promised favourably, when the Rebellion broke out and all operations were suspended.

The following sketch of the Common Schools of this period, written by Mr. Malcolm Campbell, an old teacher of Middlesex, is inserted because it is believed to be typical of Upper Canada conditions. Mr. Campbell began to teach in 1835:—

"The School Houses, during the time I taught, were built of round logs about 14 × 16 ft., with clapboard roofs and open fireplaces. A window sash on three sides for light, a board being placed beneath them, on which to keep copies and slates. There were long hewn benches without backs for seats. There were no blackboards or maps on the chinked walls. There was a miscellaneous assortment of books, which made it very difficult to form classes. Cobb's and Webster's Spelling-books afterwards gave place to Mavor's. The Testament was used as a Textbook, a supply of which was furnished by Rev. Benjamin Cronyn, afterwards Bishop of Huron. The English Reader, and Hume and Smollett's History of England were used by the more advanced classes. Lennie's Grammar, and Dilworth's and Hutton's Arithmetics, and the History of Cortez' Conquest of Mexico were used, also a Geography and Atlas, and a variety of books. Goose-quills were used for pens, which the teacher made and mended at least twice a day. The hours of teaching were somewhat longer than at present, and there was no recess. The number of scholars varied from 15 to 30, and school was kept open eight to ten months in the year with a Saturday vacation every two weeks. Teachers, after having taught school for some months, underwent a pretty thorough oral examination by the District Board of Education, and were granted First, Second, or Third Class certificates according to their merits, real or supposed. They had the Government grant apportioned to them according to their standing. Mr. Donald Currie, in the section west of me, drew annually $120 on the ground of his high qualifications as well as his teaching Latin. My share of the grant was $80. Mr. Benson east of me drew $50. . . . The Government grant was what the teacher mainly depended on for cash. The rest of his pay, which varied from $10 to $16 a month, Government grant included, was mostly paid in "kind," and very hard to collect at that.

[51] See Journals of Assembly of Upper Canada for 1837, Legislative Library, Toronto.

[52] See D. H. E., Vol. III., pp. 93-98.

"The Trustees in these early days assumed duties beyond what they now possess. In engaging a teacher, they examined him as to his qualifications in the three R's and as much farther as any of themselves knew. They fixed the rate bill which each scholar should pay, usually at a dollar and fifty cents a quarter; and any family sending more than three scholars should go free, as well as the children of widows. . . . The teacher was expected to 'board round' at that rate of pay. He usually boarded in one or two houses near the school, doing chores morning and evening. The Trustees assessed each scholar with half a cord of wood during winter, which was scantily supplied; sometimes the teacher and bigger boys went with an axe to the woods to make up the deficiency. The trustees were to examine the school quarterly, and sign the Quarterly Reports so that the teacher might draw the Government grant."[53]

The following "Rules for the Government of Common Schools" prescribed by the Board of Education for the Niagara District is taken from Gourley's "Statistical Account of Upper Canada, 1817-1822," Vol. II.; Appendix, pp. 116-119:—

> "1. The Master to commence the labours of the day by a short prayer.
>
> "2. School to commence each day at 9 o'clock and five hours at least to be given to teaching during the day, except on Saturdays.
>
> "3. Diligence and Emulation to be cherished and encouraged among the pupils by rewards judiciously distributed, to consist of little pictures and books, according to the age of the scholar.
>
> "4. Cleanliness and Good Order to be indispensable; and corporal punishment seldom necessary, except for bad habits learned at home—lying, disobedience, obstinacy and perverseness—these sometimes require chastisement; but gentleness even in these cases would do better with most children.
>
> "5. All other offences, arising chiefly from liveliness and inattention, are better corrected by shame, such as gaudy caps, placing the culprits by themselves, not permitting anyone to play with them for a day or days, detaining after school hours, or during a play afternoon, or by ridicule.
>
> "6. The Master must keep a regular catalogue of his scholars and mark every day they are absent.
>
> "7. The forenoons of Wednesday and Saturday to be set apart for Religious Instruction; to render it agreeable the school should be furnished with at least ten copies of Barrows' 'Questions on the New Testament,' and the Teacher to have one copy of the key to these questions for his own use; the teacher should likewise have a copy of Murray's 'Power of Religion on the Mind,' Watkin's 'Scripture Biography,' and Blair's 'Class Book,' the Saturday Lessons of which are well-calculated to impress religious feeling.

[53] See D. H. E., Vol. III., pp. 131, 132.

"Note.—These books are confined to no religious denomination, and do not prevent the Masters from teaching such Catechism as the parents of the children may adopt.

"8. Every day to close with reading publicly a few verses from the New Testament, proceeding regularly through the Gospels.

"9. The afternoons of Wednesday and Saturday to be allowed for play.

"10. A copy of these Rules to be affixed up in some conspicuous place in the School-room, and to be read publicly to the Scholars every Monday morning by the Teacher."

No doubt much good teaching was done in schools nominally governed by similar codes of instruction. The teacher is always the real force in a school and good teachers are never slaves to mechanical rules.

These "rules," however, suggest a form of punishment that was largely used in those days even by good teachers and has not yet been wholly banished from the schoolroom—ridicule. Here we see it offered as an improvement upon corporal punishment. It may have had its advantages over the brutal punishments sometimes inflicted in the old days, but I think Dr. Johnson was right in saying that a reasonably severe corporal punishment was better for both teacher and pupil than either "nagging" or ridicule. No doubt the systems of Bell and Lancaster were responsible for the use recommended of ridicule in the Niagara District in 1820.

One important Bill, "An Act to Provide for the Advancement of Education,"[54] became law during the session of 1839. This Bill set apart 250,000 acres of waste lands for the support of District Grammar Schools, made provision for additional schools in districts where they were needed, and provided for the erection of new buildings and assistant masters. The Bill also placed the revenue and management of these schools under the Council of King's College. In this way King's College, Upper Canada College, and the District Grammar Schools—all the machinery of higher education—were brought under central authority.

From a careful reading of a despatch[55] sent by Sir George Arthur to the Colonial Office, in connection with the Act referred to above, it seems quite clear that the land grant of 250,000 acres now set apart for District Grammar Schools was the balance of the original 549,217 acres granted by the Crown in 1798 for the endowment of Free Grammar Schools and a University. Thus, after forty years, the intentions of the Crown regarding Grammar Schools were to be realized. But only in part, because the Act of 1839 did not make the Grammar Schools free.

It was confidently hoped by many of the King's College Council, and especially by the President, Rev. Dr. Strachan, that when the college charter was amended in 1837 nothing would interfere with the immediate execution of plans for building and opening King's College. Elaborate plans and models of a building were prepared and sent out from England, an architect was employed, advertisements

[54] See Journals of Legislature of Upper Canada for 1839. Legislative Library, Toronto. See also copy of bill in D. H. E., Vol. III., pp. 170, 171.

[55] Reprinted in D. H. E. See Vol. III., pp. 173-183.

for tenders for a building were inserted in various newspapers, and the contract was about to be awarded, when Sir George Arthur hurriedly convened the Council and ordered an investigation into the finances of the College.

His suspicions had evidently been awakened by some returns on College affairs presented in response to an Address by the Assembly. The report of the special audit committee[56] appointed by the Council revealed a startling condition of affairs and incidentally a strong argument against allowing any body or corporation to handle public funds without an annual audit by someone responsible to Parliament.

The Bursar, the Hon. Joseph Wells, a prominent member of the Legislative Council, had diverted to his own use and that of his needy friends some £6,374, and the sum of £4,312 had been loaned to the President, Dr. Strachan. There was in use a very primitive system[57] of book-keeping, and on the whole just such management as might have been expected from the close corporation which had, up to 1837, made up the King's College Council. There was also much mismanagement of the financial affairs of Upper Canada College. These revelations delayed building operations until 1842.

On December 3rd, 1839, the last session of the Legislature of Upper Canada was opened by Charles Poulett Thompson, afterwards Lord Sydenham. A Bill was passed granting a charter to the "University of Kingston." When the Bill was introduced into the Assembly, the name was to be the "University of Queen's College."[58] Why the change was made does not seem very clear, but perhaps it was because the promoters of the Bill were not certain that Her Majesty had given her consent to the use of her name in the Act. The Act placed the College largely under the control of the Presbyterian Church and wholly under control of Presbyterians, but no religious tests were to be exacted from students or graduates except in Divinity. The 15th section of the charter authorized the representative of Her Majesty in Canada to pay from the revenues of King's College a sum sufficient to establish a Chair in Divinity. This arrangement doubtless was the result of a despatch from the Colonial Office some years previous to the effect that any modification of King's College charter should provide for a Divinity Professor of the Church of Scotland. Some readers of the present day may ask, Why not also for other religious denominations—Methodists, Baptists, and Congregationalists? The answer is simple. The Churches of England and Scotland were national churches in Great Britain and Ireland. The Anglican Church in Canada in 1840 claimed to be an Established Church, and as the Clergy Reserve controversy was then unsettled, her claim had reasonable expectation of realization. Had her claim been allowed, it would have strengthened any claim the Presbyterian Church might have made also to rank as an Established Church.

This Canadian charter to the "University of Kingston" was cancelled by the Crown with the consent of the Presbyterian Church in Canada, and a Royal Char-

[56] See proceedings of King's College Council, 1837-1840.

[57] See Report of T. C. Patrick, Vol. II., manuscript Minutes King's College Council, pp. 68-73.

[58] See D. H. E., Vol. III., Chap. XVI., pp. 284-299.

ter issued to the "University of Queen's College." By this Royal Charter, Queen's lost the Divinity Professorship which, by the Canadian charter, was to be established out of King's College foundation. The Crown had power to grant a charter but no power to interfere with the funds of King's College, which were subject to the Canadian Legislature.

The Commission[59] appointed by the Legislature in 1839 to prepare a report[60] on education gave a comprehensive account of the condition of schools, but without throwing much new light upon them. The total number of pupils in the District Grammar Schools was still about 300, but the number in the Common Schools was estimated at 24,000, or about one in eighteen of the total population. As to the nature of the schools attended by these 24,000, there is abundant evidence to prove that they were very inefficient. The Rev. Robt. McGill, of Niagara, says: "I know the qualifications of nearly all the Common School teachers in this district, and I do not hesitate to say that there is not more than one in ten fully qualified to instruct the young in the humblest department." The London District Board for 1839 says: "The Masters chosen by the Common School Trustees are often ignorant men, barely acquainted with the rudiments of education and, consequently, jealous of any school superior to their own."[61]

The Grammar Schools had been gradually improving since their establishment, but were still very far from supplying the real needs of the people. They had no uniformity in course of study or textbooks, and were under no inspection. In fact, lack of supervision was the weakest spot in the whole school system.

Lord Durham, in his famous Report,[62] refers to education in Upper Canada thus: "A very considerable portion of the Province has neither roads, post offices, mills, schools, nor churches. The people may raise enough for their own subsistence and may even have a rude and comfortless plenty, but they can seldom acquire wealth; nor can even wealthy landowners prevent their children from growing up ignorant and boorish, and from occupying a far lower mental, moral and social position than they themselves fill. . . . Even in the most thickly peopled districts there are but few schools, and those of a very inferior character; while the more remote settlements are almost entirely without any."

The Committee recommended better salaries, normal schools for training teachers, British textbooks, an Inspector-General of Education, and a Provincial Board of School Commissioners. Looking at the matter three-quarters of a century later, we can see that really good schools were not then immediately possible. Schools, like everything else, cannot be created at command. They are the result of evolution. Upper Canada College illustrates this. Expensive buildings were erected and capable masters secured in England, and yet the school was not really efficient for many years. The country was largely a wilderness. The people were comparatively poor and their first care was to provide the necessities of life. The sad side to the picture is that there was among the mass of the people so little real

[59] The members were: Rev. John McCaul, Rev. Henry Grasett and Secretary Harrison.

[60] See D. H. E., Vol. III., pp. 243-283. Also Appendix to Journals of Assembly for 1840.

[61] See D. H. E., Vol. III., p. 266.

[62] See Lord Durham's Report, p. 66.

interest in education and so little appreciation of its worth. People will never struggle to acquire that of which they feel no need. It seems quite clear, too, that the struggle for civil and religious freedom and equality hindered the development of a good school system. The latter could scarcely be possible before the former had triumphed. The natural leaders of the people and those who by superior attainments and education were fitted for leadership were straining every nerve and mustering every known resource to overthrow a corrupt oligarchy. Even among the spiritual leaders of the people there was no unity of purpose. Instead of working shoulder to shoulder with one another for the moral and intellectual growth of their people, they were in many cases sapping their strength through acrimonious and recriminating discussions of state church, sectarianism, Clergy Reserves, endowment and grants. When once it was finally settled that Upper Canada was to have responsible government and that all races and all creeds were to enjoy equal civil, religious and political rights, it was much easier to lay a solid foundation for the development of efficient schools.

To this nothing contributed more than the Municipal Act of 1841. It supplied the necessary local machinery, working in harmony and in close connection with a central government. It seemed to leave almost everything to local initiative and local control, thus appealing to local patriotism. In reality it gave a central authority power to direct by laying down broad general principles, and it stirred up a maximum of local self-effort by distributing Provincial grants.

Sydenham's first Speech from the Throne to the Legislature of the United Canadas in 1841 referred to the necessity of a better system of Common Schools. During the session the Legislature passed an elaborate Act for this purpose, and although it proved not to be of a practical nature it showed an earnest desire on the part of the Legislature to improve the Common Schools. The Act appropriated £50,000 per year to be distributed among the Common Schools in proportion to the number of pupils between 5 and 16 years of age in each district. It provided a Superintendent of Education for the United Canadas and prescribed his duties. It established popularly-elected Township Boards and passed certain rates to be assessed on the ratepayers.

The most significant feature of the Bill was that it contained the germ which later developed into our elaborate system of Separate Schools. Early in the session, forty petitions were presented asking that the Bible be used in the schools. There was also a petition from Rev. Dr. Strachan and the Anglican clergy asking that Anglican children be educated by their own pastors and that they receive a share of public funds for support of their schools. The Roman Catholics also petitioned against some principles of the Common School Bill then before the House.

These things will probably explain why the Bill as passed contained a clause allowing any number of dissentients (not necessarily Roman Catholics) in Township Schools to withdraw and form a school of their own, and also a clause which created for cities and incorporated towns a School Board, half of whom were Protestant and half of whom were Roman Catholic. The Catholics and Protestants might work together and maintain schools in common, or they might constitute themselves into separate committees, each committee virtually controlling its own schools.

Thus we see that while the Assembly were fighting to break down a system of sectarianism in university education, they were introducing into the Common Schools a policy that led to divisions on account of religion.

During the session of 1841, the Upper Canada Academy at Cobourg secured incorporation as Victoria College with university powers, and also a grant of £500, which later was made annual. Here, too, the Legislature was granting public money to a sectarian institution, although it should be noted that no religious tests were to be exacted of any students, and that five public officers, the President of the Executive Council, the Speakers of the two branches of the Legislature, and the Attorney-General and the Solicitor-General for Canada West were to be *ex-officio* visitors and members of the Victoria College Senate.

Early in 1842, Queen's University was opened for the reception of students. Later in the same year the corner-stone of King's College was laid with imposing ceremony by Sir Charles Bagot, the Governor-General. In 1843 the King's College professors began lectures. This gave three colleges with university powers in active operation in Upper Canada in 1843.

In May, 1842, the Governor-General appointed the Hon. Robert Jameson, Vice-Chancellor of Upper Canada, to be Chief Superintendent of Education, and the Rev. Robert Murray, of Oakville, to be Assistant Superintendent for Upper Canada. Mr. Murray was a scholarly gentleman, but possessed no special qualifications for so important an office. It seems probable that as early as 1841 Sydenham had some thought of giving the position to Ryerson. It also seems probable that Sir Charles Bagot knew of this and had some communication with Ryerson in respect to it. It is more than likely that Ryerson had been too active, both in opposing the arbitrary acts of the Legislative Council and in promoting the interests of his own Church, to be readily acceptable to His Excellency's Council, nearly all of whom were Churchmen.

It was soon discovered that the Common School Act of 1841 could never be put into operation. It had only a single merit—good intentions. In 1843 it was decided to amend it and enact a separate Bill for Upper and Lower Canada. That for Upper Canada was introduced by Hon. Francis Hincks. Speaking of the Bill[63] he says: "The principle adopted in the School Bill of 1843 is this: The Government pays a certain amount to each Township—the property in that Township pays an equal amount; or if the Councillors elected by the people choose it, double the amount. This forms the School Fund, which is divided among the school districts, the Trustees of which raise the balance of the teacher's salary by a Rate Bill on the parents of the children. The system is as simple as it is just. . . . In framing this system, gentlemen, you will observe that, as in all other instances, the late Ministry have divested the grant of all local patronage. Everything has been left to the people themselves; and I feel perfectly convinced that they will prove themselves capable of managing their own affairs in a more satisfactory manner than any Government Boards of Education or visiting Superintendents could do for them.

[63] See "Reminiscences of His Public Life," by Sir Francis Hincks, pp. 175-177. Library of Parliament, Canada.

"The new School Act provides also for the establishment in each Township of a Model School—the teacher of which is to receive a larger share than others of the School Fund, provided he gives gratuitous instruction to the other teachers in the Township, under such regulations as may be established.

"There is also provision for a Model School in each county, on a similar plan, but, of course, of a higher grade. It is left to the people themselves or their representatives in the several municipalities, to establish these Model Schools or not, as they deem expedient. But it is provided that as soon as a Provincial Normal School shall be in operation (and the system will never be complete without one) the teachers of the Model Schools must have certificates of qualification from the professors of the Normal School."

This Act of 1843 is much more elaborate in its provisions than any preceding legislation affecting Common Schools in Upper Canada. It provided for county superintendents appointed by wardens and for township, town or city superintendents appointed by the municipal council. It would seem that in many points the duties of these two classes of superintendents would conflict, as both were allowed to examine and appoint teachers, and both were to visit schools. Every section was to have a Board of Trustees elected by ratepayers, and to these trustees was given charge of school property and the regulation of course of study, including choice of textbooks. It would seem that full local control was given except in the matter of certificating teachers and regulating the government grant.

Either Protestants or Roman Catholics might petition for a Separate School on the application of ten or more resident freeholders, but such schools when established were maintained and controlled by the same machinery as other schools. Model Schools were to receive a larger grant from the Legislature. A county superintendent could issue unlimited or limited certificates, but all certificates issued by a township, town, or city superintendent were limited to the division in which they were issued and were valid for one year only.

The marked weaknesses of the Act may be summed up as follows:—

1. Possible conflict of authority between county and local superintendents.

2. No uniformity of course of study or textbooks.

3. No accepted standard of qualification for teachers.

4. No method provided for training of teachers, as a Normal School was merely suggested, and Model Schools were optional.

5. No provision made to secure competent local superintendents. Any man might be appointed.

But with all its deficiencies the School Bill of 1843 was a proof that the Legislature earnestly desired to promote elementary education. It was, no doubt, felt by many public men, and especially by the Governor, that no man was so well qualified as Ryerson to direct that system at headquarters. To pave the way for Ryerson's appointment, Rev. Robert Murray was made Professor of Mathematics in King's College, and in September, 1844, Ryerson became Assistant Superintendent of Education for Upper Canada. He was to have leave of absence for travel and for investigation into the school systems of Europe.

As events proved, Ryerson's appointment as Superintendent of Education soon bore fruit in a more efficient system of Common Schools. But university affairs were still in a state of chaos.

The amendments to the charter of King's College made in 1837 were disappointingly unfruitful of any practical changes. The College remained in charge of Anglicans, and was in reality, if not in a legal sense, a Church of England institution. The question may naturally be asked, why did the legislation of 1837 not effect greater changes? The answer is simple. In 1837 the seat of government was at Toronto, and the five *ex-officio* Government officers could easily attend meetings of King's College Council. But after the Act of Union in 1841 the seat of government was moved first to Kingston and later to Montreal. It then became wholly impossible for the five lay members of King's College to attend regular meetings in Toronto. The result was that the affairs of King's College remained practically in the hands of the president and professors, who made no real efforts to adapt the College to the needs of the people of Upper Canada. Bishop Strachan, the President, could not forget his original plans in securing the charter, and was still trying to realize them as far as possible. In a petition which he presented to Parliament in 1845 against the Draper University Bill, he makes his real object very clear. He says: "Above all things, I claim from the endowment the means of educating my clergy. This was my chief object in obtaining the Royal Charter and the Endowment of King's College; . . . and was indeed the most valuable result to be anticipated by the institution. . . . This is a point which never can be given up, and to which I believe the faith of Government is unreservedly pledged."[64] As time went on and the history of the Royal grant of 1798 came to be more fully discussed and understood, the determination of the people grew more and more fixed to secure such modifications in the King's College Charter as would make it a national instead of a sectarian institution.

The proposal of Baldwin, introduced in 1843, was statesmanlike, and although it failed to pass owing to the early resignation of his Ministry, it is interesting because it outlined in part the principles upon which the University question was finally settled. The Bill proposed to create a University of Toronto, and leave King's College as a theological seminary without power to confer degrees. Queen's, Victoria, and Regiopolis[65] were to become affiliated in connection with Toronto University, and were to surrender their powers to confer degrees. In return they were to receive certain grants from the King's College endowment. Toronto University was to become the only degree-conferring power in Upper Canada. Baldwin had the Governor's consent to bring in this Bill, and had his Ministry remained in power it would doubtless have passed. The Bill had the active support of Queen's and Victoria, and the bitter opposition of Dr. Strachan.[66]

Dr. Ryerson summed up the whole situation in a reply to an eloquent and very

[64] See D. H. E., Vol. V., p. 137.

[65] Regiopolis, a Roman Catholic college incorporated by the Legislature in 1837, had not, at this time, degree-conferring powers.

[66] See his petition presented to House of Assembly, 1843, against Bill.

able argument of Hon. W. H. Draper, who appeared at the Bar of the House of Assembly as Counsel of King's College Council, in opposition to the Bill. Dr. Ryerson concludes as follows: "The lands by which King's College has been so munificently endowed, were set apart nearly fifty years ago (in compliance with an application in 1797 of the Provincial Legislature) for the promotion of Education in Upper Canada. This was the object of the original appropriation of those lands—a noble grant, not to the Church of England, but to the people of Upper Canada. In 1827 Doctor Strachan, by statements and representations against which the House of Assembly of Upper Canada protested again and again, got 225,944 acres of these lands applied to the endowment of the Church of England College. Against such a partial application and perversion of the original Provincial objects of that Royal grant the people of Upper Canada protested; the Charter of King's College was amended to carry out the original object of the Grant; the general objects of the amended Charter have been defeated by the manner in which it has been administered, and the University Bill is introduced to secure their accomplishment; and the Council of King's College employ an advocate to perpetuate their monopoly. The reader can, therefore, easily judge who is the faithful advocate and who is the selfish perverter of the most splendid educational endowment that was ever made for any new country. . . . I argue for no particular University Bill; but I contend upon the grounds of right and humanity, that Presbyterians, Methodists and all others ought to participate equally with the Episcopalians in the educational advantages and endowments that have been derived from the sale of lands, which, pursuant to an application from the Provincial Legislature, were set apart in 1797 by the Crown for the support of Education in Upper Canada."[67]

In looking back upon the situation from our vantage-ground, covering a lapse of nearly three-quarters of a century, we may marvel that all parties were not ready to compromise upon the basis of a purely secular and national university. But secular, state-owned colleges are a very modern growth, and few men among our grandfathers had the courage to champion such institutions. An educational institution without some religious basis had uncanny associations. Therefore, it is not a matter for surprise that many good men were prepared to mutilate the University Endowment of Upper Canada, and dissipate it among sectarian colleges. Such, to a large degree, would have been the result had the Draper Bill of 1845 become law.

The Draper Government made a further attempt to settle the vexed question in 1846. John A. Macdonald (afterwards Sir John A. Macdonald) made another unsuccessful attempt in 1847. The Hon. Robert Baldwin then became Premier, and after securing the Report of a Commission on University Affairs, he introduced and passed a University Bill in 1849. This Act has been many times amended, but the final result has been to preserve for the people of Upper Canada the University Endowment, and to remove from the management every semblance of sectarian control. The University has become the property and the pride of all classes, irrespective of race, politics, or religion.

---

[67] See D. H. E., Vol. V., pp. 49-59.

CHAPTER V.

RYERSON'S FIRST REPORT ON A SYSTEM OF ELEMENTARY INSTRUCTION.

"The true greatness of a people does not consist in borrowing nothing from others, but in borrowing from all whatever is good, and in perfecting whatever it appropriates."—*M. Cousin.*

This quotation from the eminent Frenchman admirably illustrates the spirit of Ryerson's first Report[68] and the draft of proposed legislation accompanying it. His Report contains comparatively little that is original, being made up of ninety per cent. of quotations from Horace Mann's Report and from reports of eminent European statesmen and educators. And yet the Report is none the less valuable because of the quotations, nor does a reading of it tend to lessen one's respect for the writer. On the contrary, the aptness of the quotations and the skilful way in which Ryerson marshals his proofs, show his statesmanship and genius for organization. He saw enough during his European and American tours of investigation to convince him that Canada could, with profit to herself, borrow many things from other peoples. His shrewd common sense and intimate first-hand knowledge of Canadian conditions told him exactly what ought to be done, and he wisely allowed others to tell in his Report their own stories. His position was that of a skilled advocate bringing forth witness after witness to give evidence to the soundness of his theories.

He sets out by defining education, and although his definition is not scientific in a psychological sense, it is essentially correct—it points to the school as an agency to promote good citizenship. "By education I mean not the mere acquisition of certain arts or of certain branches of knowledge, but that instruction and discipline which qualify and dispose the subjects of it for their appropriate duties and employments of life, as Christians, as persons of business, and also as members of the civil community in which they live."

Ryerson then points out that in Upper Canada the education of the masses has been sacrificed to the education of a select class. He wishes to see a system of universal education adapted to the needs of the country. "The branches of knowledge which it is essential that all should understand should be provided for all,

[68] See "Report on a System of Public Elementary Instruction for Upper Canada," by Egerton Ryerson, published 1847, consisting of 191 pages.

Note.—Unless otherwise specified, all quotations in this Chapter are from the above report.

and taught to all; should be brought within the reach of the most needy and forced upon the attention of the most careless. The knowledge required for the scientific pursuit of mechanics, agriculture, and commerce must needs be provided to an extent corresponding with the demand and the exigencies of the country; while to a more limited extent are needed facilities for acquiring the higher education of the learned professions." The Report sets forth a great array of proof drawn from the United States, Britain, Switzerland, Germany, and other European countries, to show that the productive capacity of the people, their morality and intelligence, are in direct proportion to their schools and institutions of learning. Ryerson lays down as fundamental that any system adopted for Upper Canada must be universal in the sense of giving elementary instruction to all and practical in the sense of fitting for the duties of life in a young country. He goes to considerable trouble to show that in his view the practical includes religion and morality, as well as a development of the merely intellectual powers.

Ryerson was no narrow ecclesiastic, but still he could conceive of no sound system of elementary instruction that did not provide for the teaching of the essential truths of Christianity. He was decidedly not in favour of secular schools or secular colleges. And yet he believed that religious instruction in mixed classes was possible, and pointed out in his Report how it might be conducted. He made a very sharp distinction between religion and dogma, between the essential truths of Christianity and sectarianism. Dogma and sectarian teaching, in his opinion, had no place in schools except in those where all the pupils were of a common religious faith. What he pleads for in his Report is the recognition of Christianity as a basis of all instruction, and the teaching of as much of the Bible as could be given without offending any sectarian prejudices. "To teach a child the dogmas and spirit of a Sect, before he is taught the essential principles of Religion and Morality, is to invert the pyramid, to reverse the order of nature,—to feed with the bones of controversy instead of with the nourishing milk of Truth and Charity. . . . I can aver from personal experience and practice, as well as from a very extended enquiry on this subject, that a much more comprehensive course of Biblical and Religious instruction can be given than there is likely to be opportunity for doing so in Elementary Schools, without any restraint on the one side or any tincture of sectarianism on the other,—a course embracing the entire history of the Bible, its institutions, cardinal doctrines and morals, together with the evidences of its authenticity." The Report goes on to show how from Ryerson's viewpoint the absence of religious teaching in the schools of the American Union was having a damaging effect upon the moral fibre of the national life. He further illustrated by reference to what he saw in France, Germany, and Ireland, how religious instruction might be given without causing any denominational friction or unpleasantness.

After defining the aim and scope of a national system of education, and giving it a religious foundation, the Report outlines the subjects that should be taught in Elementary Schools, and illustrates in almost every case how these several subjects should be presented. While the basis of the instruction proposed is the three R's—reading, including spelling; 'riting, and 'rithmetic—yet it is remarkable to what an extent Ryerson proposed to go in "enriching" the Common School programme. Indeed, as one reads the Report he is inclined to repeat the old adage: "There is nothing new under the sun." Almost every subject introduced into Ontario schools during the last quarter of the nineteenth century, and many which yet, in the twentieth century, seem to have an insecure foothold, and are by many denominated "fads," were included by Ryerson in his memorable Report of 1846, and the arguments he uses in favour of their adoption would not seem out of place if used by an advanced educator of the present day. He pleads for music, drawing, history, civics, inductive geography, inductive grammar teaching, concrete number work, oral instruction, mental arithmetic, nature study, experimental science, book-keeping, agriculture, physical training, hygiene, and even political economy. He illustrates some German methods of teaching reading that many Ontario teachers fondly think were originated in their own country.

Ryerson from Canada, Horace Mann from Massachusetts, Sir Kay Shuttleworth from England, besides many others, about this time paid visits to Prussia, and went home to recommend the adoption of much that they saw. These men were acute observers. They recognized that the Germans had learned something that was not generally known by other teachers. How are we to explain it? Had the German teachers by accident blundered upon better *methods* of teaching than were practised by other nations? Not so. The German methods were the natural result of the German philosophy. The work of Herbart, Froebel, and other thinkers, was bearing its natural fruit, and many of the improvements introduced into the Canadian schools by Ryerson and practised by Canadian teachers, perhaps in an empirical way, were far-away echoes of principles laboriously worked out by German scholars.

Ryerson's remarks on teaching Biography and Civil Government seem almost like an echo from some modern school syllabus. "Individuals preceded nations. The picture of the former is more easily comprehended than that of the latter, and is better adapted to awaken the curiosity and interest the feeling of the child. Biography should, therefore, form the principal topic of elementary history; and the great periods into which it is naturally and formally divided,—and which must be distinctly marked,—should be associated with the names of some distinguished individual or individuals. The life of an individual often forms the leading feature of the age in which he lived and will form the best nucleus around which to collect, in the youthful mind, the events of an age, or the history of a period. . . . Every pupil should know something of the Government and Institutions and Laws under which he lives, and with which his rights and interests are so closely connected. Provision should be made to teach in our Common Schools an outline of the principles and constitution of our Government; the nature of our institutions; the duties which they require; the manner of fulfilling them; some notions of our Civil, and especially our Criminal Code."

The second part of Ryerson's Report is wholly concerned with the machinery of a System of Public Elementary Instruction for Upper Canada. The Report, after giving an outline of the various classes of schools in France and Germany, recommends for Canada a system as follows:—Common or Primary Schools for every section of a township; District Model Schools, which would correspond with the

German Real or Trade Schools; District Grammar Schools, which would correspond with the German Higher Burgher Schools and Gymnasia; and, completing all, one or more Provincial Universities. The Report also suggested that as Districts became more populous each would in time be able to support, say three Model Schools, and these might specialize, one training for agriculture, another for commercial life, and a third for mechanical or industrial life.

Normal Schools were also recommended for the training of teachers, and elaborate arguments set forth showing their benefits. The example of France, Germany, Ireland, and the United States is quoted to show how these schools would secure better teachers, and that better teachers would mean better schools. Ryerson believed that Normal Schools would elevate teaching to the rank of a profession. He believed that the people were intelligent enough to choose good teachers in preference to poor ones if the good ones were at hand. He also pointed out how a good teacher would be able to economize the child's time and advance him much faster than an indifferent teacher.

The Report then deals with the subject of textbooks. We need to remember that in Upper Canada at this time there was no control of textbooks. Each local Board or each teacher made a selection. In the majority of cases the matter regulated itself. Pupils used what they could get. With many of the people, a book was a book, and one was as good as another. The utmost confusion prevailed. There had been many complaints that some of the books used were American and anti-British in tone. By 1846 the enterprise of Canadian publishers had driven out many of the American texts, but in some districts they were still in common use.[69] In reference to this, Ryerson says: "The variety of textbooks in the schools, and the objectionable character of many of them, is a subject of serious and general complaint. All classification of the pupils is thereby prevented; the exertions of the best teacher are in a great measure paralyzed; the time of the scholars is almost wasted; and improper sentiments are often inculcated." The Report suggests that this matter must be under central control and not left to any local board or district superintendent. To fully appreciate the importance of this matter we need to remember that books meant more sixty years ago than they do to-day in any system of instruction. The better the teacher the less he is dependent upon a book, especially in such subjects as arithmetic, grammar, geography, or history. But in 1846 the teachers were in many cases wholly helpless without books. A boy went to school to "mind his book." Rote learning, working problems by a rule laid down in the book, studying printed questions and answers, were largely what was meant by "schooling." Bad as such a system was, its evils were increased when the books were especially unsuitable. Ryerson praised very highly the series in use in the National Schools of Ireland, and later he introduced them into Canada.

Public men in Upper Canada who took an interest in education had long recognized that the Common Schools were sadly in need of a stronger central control, and some system of inspection. But how to secure these safeguards and yet not

[69] A Report made to the Education Office, for 1846, shows that there were in use in Upper Canada schools 13 Spelling, 107 Reading, 35 Arithmetic, 20 Geography, 21 History, and 16 Grammar texts, besides 53 different texts in various other subjects.

destroy the principle of local control was no easy problem to solve. The township superintendents were not educators. They often were intelligent men, but as a class were without any knowledge of how to guide schools or inspire teachers to nobler things. They received from £10 to £20 a year for their services, which sum was as good as wasted. The Act of 1841, and that of 1843, had made provision for local superintendents of education, and had also defined their duties, but the Act had made no provision to secure the due performance of their orders. They were without power except such as the District and Township Boards voluntarily allowed them to assume. They might make suggestions and give advice, but with that their legal functions were at an end.

When M. Cousin, in 1836, visited Holland to examine into the system of primary instruction in that country, the Dutch Commissioner who had founded the system said to him: "Be watchful in the choice of your inspectors; they are the men who ought to be sought for with a lantern in the hand." Ryerson recognized the truth of this, and in his Report laid it down as essential to any efficient system.

His report on the control that should be exercised directly by the Government I shall quote entire.

"(1) To see that the Legislative grants are faithfully and judiciously expended according to the intentions of the Legislature; that the conditions on which the appropriations have been made are in all cases duly fulfilled.

"(2) To see that the general principles of the law as well as the objects of its appropriations are in no instance contravened.

"(3) To prepare the regulations which relate to the general character and management of the schools, and the qualifications and character of the teachers, leaving the employment of them to the people and a large discretion as to modes of teaching.

"(4) To provide or recommend books from the catalogue of which Trustees or Committees may be enabled to select suitable ones for the use of their schools.

"(5) To prepare and recommend suitable plans of school-houses and their furniture and appendages as one of the most important subsidiary means of securing good schools—a subject upon which it is intended by me, on a future occasion, to present a special report.

"(6) To employ every constitutional means to excite a spirit of intellectual activity and enquiry, and to satisfy it as far as possible by aiding in the establishment and selection of school libraries and other means of diffusing useful knowledge.

"(7) Finally and especially, to see that an efficient system of inspection is exercised over all the schools. This involves the examination and licensing of teachers, visiting the schools, discovering errors and suggesting remedies as to the organization, classification and methods of teaching in the schools, giving counsel and instruction as to their management, carefully examining the pupils, animating teachers, trustees and parents by conversations and addresses, whenever practicable, imparting vigour by every available means to the whole school system. What the Government is to the system and what the teacher is to the school, the local inspector or superintendent of schools should be within the limits of his district."

This plan made the Local Superintendent responsible for the examination and licensing of teachers according to regulations laid down by the Department. With this important exception it will be seen that the functions of the Government as exercised through the Department of Education are substantially the same to-day as they were outlined in Ryerson's first report.

The concluding part of the report dealt with what Ryerson called "Individual Efforts," and under this heading he said some very sensible things. He emphasized the importance of parents taking an interest in the school, of clergymen and magistrates visiting the school, of good school libraries, of Teachers' Institutes, of debating clubs, and of every agency that would assist in stimulating intellectual life.

CHAPTER VI.

RYERSON'S SCHOOL BILL OF 1846.

The year 1846 will ever be memorable in the annals of school legislation in Upper Canada, because it established the main principles upon which all subsequent school legislation was founded. As already pointed out, the Act of 1843 was largely a failure because it did not provide adequate machinery for the enforcement of its provisions. No important school legislation was undertaken during 1845 in anticipation of Ryerson's report. After making his report, Ryerson drafted a Bill which, with a few trifling emendations, became the Common School Act of 1846. It will assist us to an intelligent grasp of future legislation if we examine this Act with some care.

It first defined the duties of the Superintendent of Schools. He became the chief executive officer of the Government in all school matters. He was to apportion among the various District Councils (there were twenty at this time) in proportion to the school population, the money voted by the Legislature for the support of common schools (the total Legislative grant for 1846 was £20,962 to 2,736 schools) and see that it was expended according to the Act; he was to supply school officers with all necessary forms for making school returns and keep them posted as to school regulations; he was to discourage unsuitable books as texts and for school libraries and to recommend the use of uniform and approved texts; he was to assume a general direction of the Normal School when it became established; he was to prepare and recommend plans for school-houses, with proper furniture; he was to encourage school libraries, and finally he was to diffuse information generally on education and submit an annual report to the Governor-General.

The Act established the first General Board of Education.[70] It was to consist of the Superintendent of Education and six other members appointed by the Governor-General. This Board was to manage the Normal School, to authorize texts for schools and to aid the Superintendent with advice upon any subject which he should submit to it.

The Act provided for a Normal and Model School. It required each Municipal District Council to appoint a Superintendent of Schools. No qualification was fixed for the District Superintendent. It would have been useless to do so, because there were no men technically qualified for such positions. The only thing to do was trust to the District Council to choose the best man available. The District Municipal Council was also instructed to levy upon the rateable property of the District

[70] The one in existence from 1823 to 1833 was not established by Parliament but by the Lieutenant-Governor by the authority of the Imperial Government.

a sum for support of schools at least equal to the Legislative grant. They were to divide each township, town or city into numbered school sections. They were also given power by by-law to levy rates upon any school section for the purchase of school sites, erection of school buildings or teachers' residences in that section.

The District Superintendents became very important officers, and upon their learning, zeal, integrity and tact must have depended much of the success or failure of the schools of this period. They were required to apportion the District School Fund, consisting of the Legislative grant and Municipal levy, among the various school sections in proportion to the number of children between five and sixteen years of age resident in the section, and pay these sums to the teacher on the proper order being presented; to visit all schools in their Districts[71] at least once a year and report on their progress and general condition; to advise trustees and teachers in regard to school management; to examine candidates for teachers' certificates, and grant licenses, either temporary or permanent, to those who were proficient; to revoke licenses held by incompetent or unsuitable teachers; to prevent the use of unauthorized textbooks; and finally, to make an annual report of the schools in their districts to the Chief Superintendent.

The Act declared that all Clergymen, Judges of the District Court, Wardens, Councillors and Justices of the Peace were to be school visitors, with the right to visit any school or schools in their districts except Separate Schools. They were given authority to question pupils, conduct examinations and advise the teachers, or make reports to the District Superintendent. They were especially charged with the duty of encouraging school libraries. One remarkable power was conferred upon them. Any two school visitors of a district were allowed to examine a candidate for a teacher's license and grant such license if they saw fit for a term not exceeding one year in a specified school.

There are two simple explanations[72] of this clause in Ryerson's School Act. He may have wished to interest school visitors in the schools by giving them some power. He may have wished to create a local power to act in an emergency if a school became vacant through any cause during a school term. In many cases the Superintendent lived fifty to seventy-five miles from the remote corners of his District, and with the primitive means of communication in use at that time, it was an advantage to have some local body with authority to license teachers.

It is a matter for regret that at the present time the various officials mentioned here as school visitors, as well as parents generally, are so seldom seen inside the public schools. True, we now have trained teachers, and teaching has so far become a profession that few school visitors would care to question pupils, but the very presence in the school-room from time to time of educated men and women, and especially those occupying public positions, has a beneficial effect upon both teachers and pupils. Pupils feel that the work of the school must be important if it

[71] Five Districts had, in 1846, more than 200 schools each, the average for the Province being 155 schools for each District.

[72] Ryerson also gives as a reason his desire to make a gradual transition from the old system of license by Township Boards to the new plan of granting licenses only by the District Superintendent. See D. H. E., Vol. VII., P. 155.

is worthy of the attention of busy and successful men. Teachers are encouraged to make a good showing and are often hungry for the few words of sympathy and encouragement that would naturally accompany such visits. The school can never fully realize its function as a social institution unless the best citizens take an active interest in it. This was uppermost in Ryerson's mind when he penned that part of his report relating to individual efforts in promoting the welfare of the school.[73]

The Act of 1846 defined in detail how school trustees were to be elected. In all previous Acts the whole Trustee Board was elected annually. This gave to the Board no continuity of corporate life. One Trustee Board might have certain plans and make a certain bargain with a teacher. The new Board might have different plans and repudiate the contracts of its predecessor. Ryerson's Bill solved the difficulty by having trustees elected for three years, one to retire annually. Trustees' duties were not materially different from those of trustees to-day except in one or two particulars. They had to raise by a rate bill upon parents of pupils attending school such sums as were required over and above the two school grants for payment of the teacher's salary and the incidental expenses of the school; they were required to make provision by which the children of indigent parents were exempted, wholly or in part, from school rates; and they were required to select school books from a list sanctioned by the Department of Education. In Ryerson's draft bill he proposed that the rate bill should be levied upon the property of the section. This would virtually have given free schools. The Legislature of 1846 amended this clause and made the rate bill assessable only upon parents of children in actual attendance. Ryerson says of these rate bills:[74] "The evils of the present system of school rate bills have been brought under my notice from the most populous townships and by the most experienced educationists in Canada. When it is apprehended that the rate bill in a school section will be high, many will not send their children to the school at all—then there is no school; or else a few give enough to pay the teacher for three months, including the Government grant; or even after the school has commenced, if it be found that the school is not so large as had been anticipated, and that those who send will consequently be required to pay more than they had expected, parents will begin to take their children from school in order to escape the rate bill as persons would flee from a falling house! The consequence is that the school is either broken up, or the whole burthen of paying the teacher falls upon the trustees, and often as a consequence a quarrel ensues between them and the teacher. I have been assured by the most experienced and judicious men, with whom I have conversed on the subject, that it is impossible to have good schools under the present rate bill system. I think the substitute I proposed will remedy the evil. I know of none who will object to it but the rich and the childless and the selfish. Education is a public good; ignorance is a public evil. What affects the public ought to be binding upon each individual composing it. In every good government and in every good system the interests of the whole society are obligatory upon each member of it."

This rate bill, as authorized in 1846, was, however, an improvement on the old one which was levied upon parents according to the actual time of the child's

[73] See Report in D. H. E., Vol. VI., p. 208.

[74] See D. H. E., Vol. VI., p. 76.

attendance, whereas the Bill of 1846 levied a tax upon the parents of children in actual attendance for at least two-thirds of the whole school term, whether the children attended regularly or irregularly.

Teachers' duties were defined by the Act much as they are to-day. District Model Schools were authorized on the same condition as in the Act of 1843. The clauses in the Act of 1843 relating to the formation of Separate Roman Catholic or Protestant schools were also embodied in the Act of 1846.

Now, what are the distinguishing features of this School Act that reflect credit upon its author? It would be idle to pretend that there were not in Upper Canada many able men who saw the weaknesses of the school system as clearly as Dr. Ryerson. Ryerson's claim to distinction rests upon the fact that he organized a system that *worked*. He not only co-ordinated the several parts of the system, but put life into it. This was no easy task. The people were very jealous of their power of local control, and yet unless this local control could be subjected to some central control, improvement was hopeless. It was here that Ryerson did what no other man had done. He lessened local, and strengthened central, control, and did it so gradually, so wisely, and so tactfully, that local prejudices were soothed and in many cases the people scarcely recognized what was being done until the thing was accomplished. We must not suppose that all this was completed by the legislation of 1846. It began then, but its complete evolution was the work of a quarter-century.

If we ask through what agency Ryerson was enabled to secure this gradual executive strength that makes our educational machinery so effective the answer must be—the Legislative grant. The Legislature placed the grant at the disposal of the Superintendent for him to apportion among the Districts. Here was a lever of wonderful power, and Ryerson was quick to perceive its possibilities. If Districts wished a grant they must conform to certain requirements. If school sections wished a grant from the District Superintendent, they, too, must satisfy certain requirements as to textbooks, qualified teachers, building and equipment.

No doubt the Prussian system gave Ryerson many hints on this subject, but he knew that the Canadian spirit was very different from the docile German spirit fostered by generations of benevolent paternalism. I think, too, there can be no reasonable doubt that he received many practical hints on this point from the workings of Her Majesty's Committee on Education formed by the Imperial Parliament. The history of the world presents no more significant illustration of how an outside body may come to exercise an effective control over various kinds of schools than is presented by the history of the schools of Great Britain and Ireland and their control by Her Majesty's Government through parliamentary grants.

That the leaders of Canadian public opinion in the years following 1846 saw all that was involved in Ryerson's gradual strengthening of central control of educational affairs is made abundantly clear by the leading editorials in the press of that period. The Toronto *Globe*, which had been established in 1844 by the Browns, was already in 1846 the leading exponent of advanced liberal ideas in Upper Canada. As the *Globe* had been bitterly opposed to Lord Metcalfe, and had resented Ryerson's defence of him, it was not to be expected that Ryerson's appointment as

Superintendent of Education would be satisfactory to that journal, or that his educational plans would be leniently criticised. Indeed, the *Globe* editor's first objection to Ryerson's Bill of 1846 was to the great powers conferred upon the Superintendent and to the irresponsible nature of his Commission. The following is from a *Globe* editorial of April 14th, 1846;[75] "We have read a draft of the new School Bill for Upper Canada brought in by Mr. Draper. We have not been able to go over all its claims, but it contains one objectionable principle, viz.: the appointment and dismissal of the Superintendent is vested in the Governor-General personally and not in the Governor-General with the advice of his Council, as it ought to be. The whole funds from which the school system is to derive support are raised by the people of Canada, and the disposal of them should be subjected to the control of the House through the Executive Council. . . . The powers of the Superintendent are very great and embrace many points such as the selection of proper books, etc. A Board of seven Commissioners to assist the Superintendent is named, but the Governor may appoint them, or not, and the Superintendent may take their advice, or not, and he has also power to prevent interference at any time, for he is only to receive advice on all measures which he may 'submit to them.' The whole of this extensive institution, if the Bill passes, will be lodged in the Governor-General personally and in the Superintendent, and they may work it for any purpose that suits their views." On July 14th, 1846, the editor of the *Globe* again criticises the School Bill, because the Superintendent reports to the Governor and not to the Governor-General-in-Council.

These articles are interesting and important. Why was Ryerson's appointment vested in the Governor and not in the Executive Council? The answer not only throws valuable light upon the way that Ryerson himself viewed his office and its relation to the public, but it incidentally shows how imperfectly responsible government was established in Upper Canada in 1846. We should gasp with astonishment in Canada to-day if it were proposed to vest the appointment of any public officers in the Governor-General personally. We allow our Governors no personal freedom in the conduct of public affairs. But in 1846 that idea was not wholly accepted. There still lingered a feeling that the Crown had certain vaguely-defined prerogatives, which might be exercised without let or hindrance from Councillors. And many who recognized that the British Crown had little individual freedom of action in public affairs in Britain could not see that the same status ought to be established for the Crown's representative in a colony. Or, to put it in another way, the people did not see how a colony could be self-governing without being wholly independent.

Ryerson wished his appointment to be vested in the Governor, rather than in the Executive Council, because he thought that by such an arrangement he was a servant of the country and not of any political party. He thought that a Superintendent of Education ought, like a judge, to be placed beyond the accidents and turmoil of politics. No doubt that was an illogical position. Indeed, time showed it to be so, and that full recognition of the principle of responsible government required a Minister of Education responsible directly to the Legislature. We can only

[75] See bound volume of *Globe* in Legislative Library, Toronto.

speculate as to what would have been the effect upon our schools had Ryerson's position been looked upon as political and had he been forced to vacate his office with every change of government. It seems doubtful whether our schools would have improved as rapidly as they did under the conservative, but truly progressive, policy of Ryerson.

There is abundant evidence that there were many in Upper Canada who wished to see the position of Superintendent closely connected with politics. A *Globe* editorial, Jan. 6th, 1847, commenting on Ryerson's report, says: "We expected that when our new Superintendent stepped into his ill-gotten office he would immediately take measures to make himself acquainted with the replies to such questions as the following: First, the situation, condition and number of schools and school-houses of all kinds in the Province. Second, the manner in which school trustees, town, county and district Superintendents had discharged their several duties. Third, the desire manifested by parents generally for the education of their children. Fourth, the competency and efficiency of the teachers, their salaries, etc. Fifth, the kind of school books used, the school libraries and other apparatus for teaching. Had such questions been proposed and answered, the Superintendent would have had something to base a report upon. It was but natural to suppose that an officer whose sole prospects of success are in the confidence and co-operation of the people would have taken some steps to gain that confidence and co-operation, that he would have been desirous by direct communication with superintendents, trustees, experienced teachers and influential persons in the Province of ascertaining their views and of obtaining their suggestions as to the best means of promoting the interests of the noble department over which he had been called to preside. But no, it is true he was devising a system of education for Canada, but what had the wants or wishes of the people to do with it? The serfs must receive anything I, their lord and master, may import from the cringing subjects of despotic monarchies. We are more and more convinced from the examination of this report that Mr. Ryerson is not competent for the situation which he occupies."

This is manifestly unfair. Ryerson knew from previous experience and without any further special investigation, the answer to every one of the five questions propounded above. In 1848, just after the Baldwin-Lafontaine administration was formed, and before the newly-formed ministry had met Parliament, there was more or less discussion about dismissing Ryerson from his position as Superintendent of Education. The *Globe* of April 29th, 1848, says: "Will any man, except a few of his own clique, say that Egerton Ryerson should be Superintendent of Education under a Liberal Government? We apprehend none. He has done nothing wrong since his appointment, it is said. We say he has. He spent many months on the Continent of Europe and in Britain in amusement or recreation, professing to get information about things which every person knew already. . . . We have had hints of the Prussian system being applicable to Canada and we feel convinced that he, who sold himself to the late Administration, would have readily brought all the youth of Canada to the same market and placed them under the domination of an arbitrary and coercive power. He had sold their fathers for pelf, why not sell the sons also? Was he not in league with that party which would retain the Province in vassalage to the old Compact which he had so heartily denounced in former times? Is he not a member of that Methodist Committee which bargained away to a worthless Ministry the Methodist votes for £1,500 to Victoria College? These are most memorable events in the annals of political corruption. . . . But we care not if there had been no ground for complaint since 1844. We know that Egerton Ryerson sold himself body and spirit to Lord Metcalfe and that he broached doctrines of the most unconstitutional kind, threatening those who were but asking the common rights of British subjects with the vengeance of the whole Empire. The man who holds such views is unfit to be at the head of the country's education. He would convert the children of the Province into the most pliable tools of an arbitrary system."

These articles show clearly that the party press was not disposed to judge Ryerson by his work as Superintendent of Education. They claimed that because he championed Lord Metcalfe in 1844 he was a partizan, and if a partizan in 1844 he must still be one in 1848.

Besides a certain amount of political prejudice, Ryerson had to overcome the many points of friction caused by an attempt to work the Bill of 1846, and when we consider the ignorance and incompetence among those upon whom the administration of the Act rested, and the prejudices against the Act by many who were supremely selfish, we have to admit that a less courageous man would have utterly failed. Many trustees could neither read nor write. In some cases the District Municipal Councillors who were parties to school administration were equally ignorant. District Superintendents of schools were not always fitted for such a responsibility. Perhaps half the whole body of teachers made up a motley assortment of impecunious tramps. The Superintendent's report for 1847 shows that out of 2,572 schoolhouses only 133 were of brick or stone, and that 1,399 were made of logs; 1,378 had no playground, and only 163 were provided with water-closets. With many superintendents, trustees, and teachers miserably incompetent, with buildings and equipment woefully inadequate, it required a stout heart to undertake a reformation.

Ryerson had two temperamental qualities that stood him in good stead; he had an idealist's faith in humanity, believing that men would choose the higher if it could once be shown them; he had besides an infinite capacity for hard work and for taking pains. This is fully shown by the way he met the many objections to his Bill of 1846. The bitterest opposition came from the Council of the Gore District, now the County of Wentworth, a District from which more progressive ideas might have been expected. On the 10th November, 1846, this Council[76] petitioned the Legislative Assembly against Ryerson's Bill. They objected to a Provincial Board of Education and to a Chief Superintendent. They wished to have re-enacted the School Bills of 1816 and 1820. Among other things the petition says: "With respect to the necessity of establishing a Normal, with elementary Model Schools in this Province, your memorialists are of opinion that however well adapted such an institution might be to the wants of the old and densely populated countries of Europe, where service in almost every vocation will scarcely yield the common

[76] See copy of petition in D. H. E., Vol. VII., pp. 114-116.

necessaries of life, they are altogether unsuited to a country like Upper Canada, where a young man of such excellent character as a candidate is required to be to enter a Normal School and having the advantage of a good education besides, need only turn to the right hand or to the left to make his service much more agreeable and profitable to himself, than in the drudgery of a common school, at an average of £29 per annum [the average in Upper Canada for 1845]; nor do your memorialists hope to provide qualified teachers by any other means in the present circumstances of the country than by securing as heretofore the services of those whose physical disabilities from age render this mode of obtaining a livelihood the only one suited to their decaying energy, or by employing such of the newly-arrived immigrants as are qualified for common school teachers, year by year as they come amongst us, and who will adopt this as a means of temporary support until their character and abilities are known and turned to better account for themselves."

This petition was sent to every District Council in Upper Canada. Some districts agreed with it, some were indifferent and some wholly opposed its spirit. Colborne District Council took a very different attitude. They praised the Chief Superintendent, warmly approved of a Normal School, and found much to admire in the legislation of 1846. The following from their report will serve as an illustration:[77] "As the Normal and Model Schools begin to yield their legitimate fruits, and as the blighting effects of employing men as school teachers who are neither in manners nor in intellectual endowments much above the lowest menials, shall press less and less heavily upon the mental and moral habitudes of the rising generation, the great benefits to be derived from the present Common School Act, and its immense superiority over all former school laws of Upper Canada, will become more and more confessed and appreciated. Already that public apathy which is the deadliest enemy to improvement is slowly yielding to the necessity imposed by the present school law upon the trustees and others of acquiring extended information, of entering with a deeper interest into all matters connected with Common Schools and of joining with school visitors, superintendents and municipal councillors in a more active and vigilant oversight of them."

Ryerson saw that public opinion must be educated. The problem was a wider one than the education of the rising generation in the schoolhouses. The fathers and mothers and all who made public opinion must be awakened. This work Ryerson did in a characteristic manner. He had been a missionary preacher of the Gospel; he now became an educational missionary. He sent carefully-prepared circulars to Municipal Councils, to District Superintendents, to school trustees and to teachers. He established at his own financial risk, and without accepting a penny of the profits for his labour, an educational journal as a means of communication with the general public. In the autumn of 1847 he spent ten weeks in visits to the twenty-one Districts into which Upper Canada was at that time divided. He called District Educational Conventions, lasting each two days. To these were invited teachers, District Superintendents, School Visitors, Municipal Councillors and the general public. The Warden was generally secured as chairman. During the day,

[77] See copy of memorial in D. H. E., Vol. VII., p. 117.

Ryerson discussed the School Act and its operation. He found that often the people had been misled and that trustees who had never made any attempt to enforce the Act had laid the blame for their poor school upon the Act of 1846. In almost every case a frank discussion face to face with the parties concerned removed unreasonable prejudices and made friends for the new Superintendent. In the evening, Ryerson gave a public lecture. His subject in 1847 was "The Advantage of Education to an Agricultural People." No subject could have been more appropriate to secure the sympathy of the mass of the people and to give the lecturer an opportunity to show what he hoped to do for Upper Canada.

CHAPTER VII.

THE RYERSON BILL OF 1850.

The Act of 1846 provided that the Municipal Councils of Toronto and Kingston were to have the same powers in school matters as the District Councils. Toronto had at this time twelve school sections, each with its own Trustee Board, and each fixing its own textbooks and course of study. Such a system was cumbersome, wasteful, and inefficient, and the practical mind of Ryerson devised a remedy. In 1847, the Cities and Towns Act was passed. This Act required the Municipal Councils of cities and towns to appoint a School Board of six members. These six, together with the Mayor of the Corporation, had full control of all schools and school property. They could determine the number and kind of schools and the texts to be used, but they had no power either to levy an assessment upon property or to collect rate bills from parents. Any funds needed by the School Board in addition to the Legislative and Municipal grants were to be levied upon the taxable property of the city or town by the Municipal Council. But the Act did not say that the Municipal Council must grant the sums asked for by the Board of Trustees. In Toronto the Council of 1848 refused to levy the necessary assessment, and the School Trustees were compelled to close the schools from July to December.

The Toronto *Globe*[78] declared that Ryerson was introducing a Prussian despotism into Canada. Ryerson said that he desired nothing Prussian in the Canadian schools except the method of schoolroom instruction, and claimed that his new School Bill was almost a literal transcript of that in force in the State of New York. Ryerson then set forth the chief advantage of the new Bill, viz.: that it gave to the poor man the *right* to have his children, however numerous, educated, whereas the rate bill system compelled him in many cases to claim free schooling only on the ground of his poverty. The new School Act was to enable a poor man to educate his children and still maintain his self-respect. The school tax was to be levied not upon the children of the section, but upon the real property. Ryerson concluded as follows: "Wealthy selfishness and hatred of the education of the poor and labouring classes may exclaim against this provision of the law, but enlightened Christian philanthropy and true patriotism will rejoice at its application."

Commenting on Ryerson's letter, the following issue of the *Globe* said: "The Doctor makes a great fuss about the cruel position of a man who cannot 'brook to say he was a pauper' under the old system and the delightful and 'enlightened Christian philanthropy' of his new system which 'places the poor man and his children upon equal footing with the rich man and his children.' All bunkum, Dr.

[78] See editorial, Toronto *Globe* of May 8th, 1848.

Ryerson. If it is hard to have ten or fifty or one hundred scholars as paupers at present, will it improve the matter to make the children of the common schools all paupers? If one class keep their children away now because the schools are above their means, and pride won't let them submit to state the fact to a trustee, will there not hereafter be a much larger class whose pride will prevent them sending their children to what even Dr. Ryerson admits will be pauper schools?. . . Is it not melancholy that so crooked, so visionary a man as this should be at the head of the literary institutions of the country?"

But Ryerson was fighting for free schools. He knew that thousands of children were growing up ignorant, especially in the large towns. He was able to show that in the city of Toronto, out of 4,450 children of school age in 1846, only 1,221 were on the common school registers and that the average attendance was scarcely one thousand. Even if it were granted that another thousand were in attendance at private and church schools, the fact remained that not more than half the children in Toronto were being educated.

In October, 1848, Ryerson submitted to the Government a draft School Bill, designed to remedy the defects in the legislation of 1846-1848. In a report[79] which he submitted with his draft Bill he says: "No law which contemplates the removal of grovelling or selfish ignorance and the elevation of society by means of efficient regulations and general taxation for schools ever has been, or ever will be, popular with the purely selfish or the listlessly ignorant. All such laws must be sustained for a time at least by the joint influence of the Government and the intelligent and enterprising portion of the community."

The outcry against free schools and taxation of property to educate the children of the poor showed clearly that the time had not yet come for the realization of his plans, and Ryerson in his draft Bill restored to towns and cities the right to impose rate bills upon parents, at the same time declaring his faith in the ultimate triumph of free schools.

In February, 1849, Ryerson submitted additions to his draft Bill of the previous October. Among other changes he recommended additional Superintendents for Districts of more than 150 schools; District Boards of Examiners who would replace the District Superintendent and school visitors[80] in issuing teachers' certificates; Teachers' Institutes for lectures and professional training of teachers; provision for separate schools for coloured children; school libraries for each section, and also township libraries; township School Boards; a School of Art and Design, connected with the Normal School; provincial certificates for Normal School graduates; making trustees personally responsible for a teacher's salary; the distribution of school funds on a basis of actual attendance, rather than on the number of children in the section; better provision for fixing school sites; more equitable division of the $200,000 legislative grant between Upper and Lower Canada, and provision for the admission into the common schools of pupils from sixteen to

[79] See copy in D. H. E., Vol. VIII., p. 85.

[80] The report of the Bathurst District Superintendent for 1848 showed 82 teachers certificated by School Visitors and 42 by the District Superintendent. See Report of Chief Superintendent for 1848.

twenty-one years of age.

The Baldwin Government entrusted the handling in the Legislature of the School Bill of 1849 to the Honourable Malcolm Cameron. It should be borne in mind that the Legislature met in Montreal and that the Education Office for Upper Canada was in Toronto. Dr. Ryerson was, therefore, not in direct communication with the Government, nor was he officially informed from day to day as to the progress of the Bill. It should further be borne in mind that during this session the Parliament Buildings were burned, the Governor-General mobbed, and party feeling strongly aroused, thus creating conditions favourable for hasty and careless legislation. It seems to have been taken for granted by the Legislature that the Bill as brought in was prepared by Ryerson. As a matter of fact, Ryerson's Bill had, with Cameron's assent, been so mutilated by an enemy of the Superintendent that its essential provisions were destroyed. As soon as Ryerson learned its real nature, he protested on several grounds, but especially because it aimed to destroy the usefulness of the Chief Superintendent; excluded clergymen from being school visitors; destroyed the provincial nature of the school system; injured the prospects of a Normal School; would subject teachers to serious loss in collecting their salaries; re-established school sections in towns and cities; made no provision for uniform textbooks, and because it was cumbersome and unworkable. After an elaborate analysis of the Bill, Ryerson intimated that he would not attempt to administer the law as passed and that sooner than do so he would resign. The Government soon ascertained that the Bill was unsatisfactory to everybody and intimated to Ryerson that it would not be brought into operation. This course was followed, and in the meantime Ryerson perfected his plans for a new Bill to go before the Legislature in 1850.

As the Cameron Act of 1849 was never given effect, it has no interest for us, except in so far as it shows the evolution of the Act of 1850. During the Parliamentary recess, 1849-50, the Government issued circular letters to School Superintendents, ministers and other official persons, to secure suggestions as to school legislation. The replies were handed to Dr. Ryerson by the Hon. Francis Hincks, who had charge of the School legislation for 1850.

Ryerson's draft of the Bill of 1850 is a tribute to his practical common sense and is sometimes called the Charter of the Ontario School System. Ryerson knew the people of Upper Canada as few knew them, and he was quick to see the dividing line between that which seemed highly desirable and that which was possible. He moved steadily toward a distant goal, but was ever educating public opinion to move with him and seldom showed impatience over the slow pace of travel, so long as there was actual progress. He wished to see free schools, but in this Act contented himself with securing permissive legislation, which he believed would soon lead to the adoption of a free system.

The outstanding feature of the Act was the strengthening of Trustee Boards by recognizing them as corporate bodies with full power to manage schools under Government regulations and full power to levy taxes or rates upon the District which they represented. In case the Municipal Council collected school money, they did it only as a matter of convenience. Provision was made for securing school sites, erecting and furnishing new buildings, electing trustees, holding board meetings, keeping schools accounts, appointing collectors for school moneys, providing books and apparatus, educating indigent children and forming school libraries. Teachers' duties and responsibilities were not materially altered. They were, however, effectually secured against loss of the full amount of salary promised them by trustee boards. Adequate provision was made for school sections composed of adjoining parts of two or more townships. Provision was made for Township Boards of Trustees on the request of a majority of the school supporters, to manage all the schools of a township. County Boards of Public Instruction were formed, consisting of the County Superintendent and the Trustees of the District Grammar School. These boards were to meet four times a year, to hold examinations and license teachers. They were to use their influence to establish school libraries and promote the cause of education. District superintendents were limited to one hundred schools each, and were to receive one pound per annum for each school, besides necessary travelling expenses. The Superintendent was no longer the custodian of school money, but gave orders to the Township Treasurer to pay to teachers their proper allowances. The Superintendent was to visit every school in his District once each quarter, and to deliver a public lecture in every school section once each year. Thus the way was open for the District Superintendent to become an expert, giving a minimum of time to clerical work and a maximum to the encouragement of pupils and teachers. He was to become a link between the Department of Education on the one hand and the District Council and Trustee Boards on the other. He was a local officer, but his duties were definitely prescribed by a central authority. Through him the Chief Superintendent and the Council of Public Instruction were able to keep in touch with pupils, teachers, school visitors, trustee boards, county boards, and district councils. School visitors were given the same privileges as by the Act of 1846, except the right to grant licenses to teachers. The General Board of Education was merged into the Council of Public Instruction, with duties substantially the same as those assigned the former body in 1846.

Incorporated towns and cities were no longer to have school sections, but instead a Board of Trustees to manage school affairs. Town and City School Boards were allowed three ways of securing the money necessary, in addition to the school fund, for common school purposes. The Board might ask the Municipal Council to levy an assessment for the required sum, in which case the said Council were bound to comply with its wishes; the Board might levy a rate bill upon the parents of pupils attending school; or they might raise the required funds partly by a rate bill and partly by an assessment levied by the Municipal Council.

The only real difference between the methods of raising money in towns and cities on the one hand and rural sections on the other, lay in the plan of deciding how the money was to be raised. In rural sections the ratepayers assembled at the annual meeting, made the decision, and the trustees carried out their wishes; in towns and cities the trustees had full power to decide upon the method of taxation without consulting the ratepayers. School trustees in incorporated villages were governed by the same rules as trustees of towns and cities, except in the manner of the annual election.

One very important feature of the new Act was the setting apart of £3,000 a year for the establishment and support of school libraries, and £25 a year for each District Teachers' Institute. A sum was also set apart for procuring plans and publications for the improvement of school architecture. The Chief Superintendent was authorized to issue provincial certificates to Normal School graduates.

The Act of 1850 also made some important changes relating to Separate Schools, which will be noted in another chapter.

Dr. Ryerson always felt that he owed much to the Governor-General, Lord Elgin, for helping him to form a public opinion which made possible the legislation of 1850. That distinguished nobleman was a graduate of Oxford, and he never lost an opportunity of helping forward any movement designed to raise the intellectual status of the people. But it was largely Ryerson's unaided efforts that gave Upper Canada in 1850 such a splendid educational machinery. It was no factory-made plan, but a system developed step by step out of partial failures into something better. It was, like all English law, the result of applying a common-sense remedy to a clearly proved weakness.

During the passage through the Legislature of the Bill of 1850, a debate arose about Ryerson's salary, and the value of his services to the country. The following condensed account of a speech delivered in Parliament in July, by Hon. Francis Hincks, makes clear the attitude finally adopted by the Liberal Government toward Ryerson, and for that reason has some historical interest:

> "The member for Toronto, Mr. Boulton, had charged the Administration with buying the support of the Superintendent of Education with an increased salary. He had desired, in bringing forward this question, to make it as little a political question as possible. He thought that the great question of education might be treated without reference to party differences. He thought it his duty, considering the position which the Reverend Superintendent of Education occupied towards the party with whom he acted, to state his whole course of conduct towards that gentleman since he had taken office. It was well known to the House that the reverend gentleman was engaged, before accepting the office which he now held, in very keen controversy with the members of the present ministry; he had taken a course decidedly hostile to them. As writer for the public press at that time, he had himself engaged in that contest, though without personal feeling, as he trusted he had engaged in every contest of the kind. But there was undoubtedly on his own part, and on that of his colleagues, a strong political feeling of dislike to the reverend gentleman, on account of the formidable opposition with which they were met by him. He was appointed to the office of Superintendent by the late Government, and he did not blame that Government for so appointing him; for, if anyone ever established strong

claims upon a party, it was the reverend gentleman by his defence of that administration. The present ministry again assumed the duties of the Government, and undoubtedly there was a general feeling among their supporters that one of the first measures expected of them was to get rid of the reverend gentleman in some way or other, and in that feeling most certainly he sympathized. He had found, however, bye-the-bye, that those who were most eager to recommend the Government to dismiss officials, when they were put into similar situations, into the municipal councils for instance, that they did not carry out those views, that they did not turn out their opponents without a reason for it. There were two or three ways of removing the Chief Superintendent; one was to make the office a political one; but after the best consideration being given to the question, it was not considered advisable to do that, and the proposition to abolish the office altogether, he was satisfied would have had the worst possible consequences on the educational interests of the country, after observing the benefits of active superintendents in New York, and our own Province. The only other mode then, if these two were resisted, was to remove the incumbent altogether, and then the question came, whether he had acted in such a manner as to justify his dismissal. He had often asked this question of the persons who urged his dismissal, and they had never given one good reason to support the affirmative. He was not one of those who thought that because a person supported one Government that he was therefore incapable of serving faithfully those who succeeded them, whom he had formerly opposed, always supposing, of course, that his office was not a political one. He could not find that the reverend gentleman had entered in the slightest degree into the field of politics, and as he had discharged his duties with great zeal and ability, they had no reason to interfere with him. Then the point was, how they were to act towards him in his position, and his (Mr. H.'s) determination was to give him the most cordial support; as a member of the Government he considered it his duty to do so. He felt it his duty to give the same support to officers who came oftener into contact with him, the officials of the Custom House, and he defied anyone to say that any political opponent of his had received less cordial support in the discharge of the duties of his office than his friends had; the efficiency of the service absolutely required that he should do so. He put himself in communication with the reverend gentleman in reference to this Bill, and as he (Mr. H.) believed that Doctor Ryerson possessed a more complete knowledge of the school system than any other person, he thought that any Government would have done very wrong not to have availed themselves of that knowledge. He deeply regretted the course which some gentlemen with whom he generally acted had taken on this matter.

> "He would only say now, that he considered he should be paid the highest salary given to any officer, for the duties of none were more onerous or more important. He might remark that he had not found lawyers in the House very anxious to reduce the salaries of the judges, but when it came to civilians, to superintendents of schools, then five hundred pounds a year was far too much. Now he considered the duties of that office as quite equal in importance, and requiring equal talents to those of a Collector of Customs, and thought that he should not be placed in an inferior position to them."[81]

The Toronto *Globe*, of July 16th, 1850, speaking on the debate in the Assembly, said:

> "The debate on Egerton Ryerson's salary was, we think, just another instance of pandering to the cry of the moment. His salary was sought to be made the same as the Lower Canada Superintendent's. Well, the Lower Canada Superintendent's salary is five hundred pounds, but it would not do to name that sum for Upper Canada until the retrenchment committee had operated upon Lower Canada. Now, why not say at once that five hundred pounds is the proper salary for the Superintendent of Education of nearly a million people, and stick to it? We are no admirers of Egerton Ryerson, and we have always thought, and we think still, that the present ministry should have turned him out neck and crop the moment they got into power; but we are free to admit that he is a man of very great talent, who, at any mercantile or professional business he might engage in, would readily make five hundred pounds a year, and we do think that this sum is as little as could be assigned to an office of such high public importance."

This article clearly shows that the *Globe* recognized Ryerson's talents and his professional ability, while objecting to him on political grounds. Mr. George Brown, the *Globe* Editor, was too shrewd a man, and had too strong an interest in popular education, not to see that Ryerson was working a reformation in school affairs. The following from a *Globe* editorial of September 14th, 1850, is really a tribute grudgingly paid to Ryerson's efforts:—

> "While other professions, the clergy, the lawyers, the physicians, have long gained a certain position and influence in society, and have assumed the management of their own affairs, teachers, as a class, have, until lately, stood alone, disregarded by the community, and in many instances treated as beneath the notice of men infinitely their inferiors in mental acquirements, and engaged in pursuits certainly not more important to the well-being

[81] See issue of Toronto *Globe*, July 11th, 1850, p. 331.

of the community. While others were improving their circumstances and acquiring wealth and power, the schoolmaster alone appeared stationary, doomed to drag on a life of poverty and contempt, and looked upon by parents as a sort of nurse for their naughty children, who received their wages for their services, and not to meddle with the affairs of the world. We but repeat what we wrote some years ago, prior to any of Egerton Ryerson's schemes, when we say that it is a reproach to the Christian world, that those who prepare the rising generation for entry into business life, should have been left so long to poverty, and to have occupied so low a place in society. Only conceive a schoolmaster—profoundly versed in the vast variety of knowledge which the human mind can master, a man who can solve the most difficult problem in mathematics, and take the highest flights in astronomy—rarely reaching beyond the mark of a person to be patronized. To such a man, the constant toil and drudgery of a school, the annoyance of unruly children and unreasonable parents, and above all the pinching poverty to which he is too often subject, present a life of hardship which it is difficult to conceive. The smith, or the carpenter of the village, may by industry realize something for the wants of a surviving family, and the shopkeeper, or the baker, may perhaps become wealthy; but the idea of a schoolmaster having any other position than poverty, would be thought the height of absurdity."

Ryerson believed that if school trustees were given the option of free schools and power to enforce taxation for their support, they would soon abolish rate-bills upon parents. Public sentiment was rapidly changing. This was fairly shown by the city of Toronto, where there were many wealthy men who objected to free schools, and where private and denominational schools were more popular than in any other part of Upper Canada. In March, 1851, a committee of the Toronto Board submitted to the Chairman a special report showing that 3,403 children who should be in the schools of that city were roaming the streets and growing up without educational advantages of any kind. The report ascribed this condition of affairs mainly to two causes, rate-bills and lack of school accommodation, and concluded by making a strong stand for free schools.

The Toronto *Globe* had scoffed at free schools in 1848. The rapid change that took place in the views of this journal is a fair index of the change that was taking place among the people of Upper Canada in regard to free schools. I shall, therefore, quote from the *Globe* to show the trend of public opinion on free schools during the early fifties. As early as January 30th, 1851, the *Globe* said editorially:

"We are glad to observe that the plan of free common schools has been adopted at the recent annual meetings in very many school sections throughout Upper Canada. The best gift the people of Canada can confer on their children is education, sound, practical education available to all. Public money employed in educating the masses is a most profitable investment, and we hope the day will soon be when a good education is open to every child in the country."

On January 5th, 1852, the *Globe* expressed itself as follows:—

"The most important change proposed in our present system of common schools, is the abolition of all direct charges against the parents of the children attending, and the support of these institutes by direct tax on the whole body of the people. We trust the day is not far distant when the Reserve and Rectory lands will be devoted to the support of the common schools of Upper Canada, the school tax abolished, and the unspeakable advantages of a sound education placed without any charge within the reach of every child in the Province. Every effort should be put forth to effect this, but meantime let us seek to obtain the best system which our position admits of, and that, we believe, is an entirely free system supported by a direct tax. There are many reasons urged against this proposed change by sincere friends of education, which are not without weight. It is said to be unjust and tyrannical to make people who are childless pay for those who are blessed with a numerous progeny; it is urged that parents will value the blessing of education more, when they are compelled to pay for it; it is alleged to be a weakening of the parental tie, to take the expense of the education of the child from the shoulders of the parent. These arguments will have more or less influence according to the position and character of the individual who considers them, but we assert without fear of contradiction that all the evils which our warmest opponents anticipate from the introduction of free schools sink into insignificance beside the frightful consequences of our children growing up in the blindness of ignorance, the result which a free system is designed to avert. No reasonable disinterested man would place the one class of evils in comparison with the other. . . .

"Many opponents of free schools, however, are willing that the children of the poor should be educated without charge, as they are at present. Most parents, however, would be, and are, prevented by their pride from taking advantage of this favour, and we think it highly desirable that the idea of begging education, or anything else, should be set as far as possible from the mind of every Canadian. The children of the poor should look to the common schools as a place to which they have a right to go, having paid a quota of the expense in proportion to their means, in the same way that they claim the right to walk the pavement, and on the same grounds. It is indeed a noble thought to place the education of the people in the same position as the protection of the people and the government of the people, to make it one of the

> necessaries of the existence of a state in peace and security, and to provide it at the expense of all, for the benefit of all. With a Government formed as ours is by the people, and entirely under its control, our only safeguard against anarchy and confusion is the intelligence and right of the people. A thorough system of common school education is the only means which can ensure these high advantages. Education ought to be universal, and to be so, it must be entirely free from all expense; there must be inducements held out to the short-sighted, unwilling parent."

As I have already shown, free schools had stronger opposition in Toronto than at any other point, yet at a large public meeting held in January, 1852, in St. Lawrence Hall,[82] there were only twelve people who opposed a motion for free schools. Later in the same month Doctor Ryerson himself attended a public meeting in Toronto and discussed the free school issue. I shall quote from his speech[83] to show how skilfully he could use a concrete illustration to influence public opinion. "Speaking of free schools he said he well remembered how he went to visit one of the public schools of Boston, the High School, where boys were prepared for College, yet as free of expense to all classes as the lowest, and the Mayor of the city, who accompanied him, wishing to give a lesson in aristocracy, probably, pointed out two lads who occupied the same seat. He told him that one of these was the son of Abbot Lawrence, the great manufacturer, and now American minister in England, and the other was the son of the doorkeeper of the City Hall, which they had just left. They were enjoying the same advantages, the son of the millionaire and the son of the doorkeeper; that was what he wished to see in Canada, the sons of our poor have the same opportunity of educational advancement as those of the rich. Did it appear from this that the rich did not attend the common schools of Massachusetts? The Governor of that State, in a speech which he made lately at Newbury Port, said that if he had as many sons as old Priam, and was as rich as Astor, that he would send them to the free school. There were rich and proud men in Massachusetts, undoubtedly, who would not send their children among the poor, and rich stingy men who objected to be taxed for other people's children, but they were the exceptions to the rule. There was one fact that he wished to mention in connection with the free schools of Massachusetts. A body of European clergy belonging to the Catholic Church had gone to their Bishop in Boston to request him to use his influence against the free school system. He returned for answer that he knew the character of the schools, having been educated in them, and having owed to them his position in the Church and the world, and would do nothing to impair their usefulness."

It would be a mistake to suppose that there were not valiant champions against the free school principle, and it would be a worse mistake to suppose that all the sound arguments were on the side of free schools. The following letters from the Reverend John Roaf, a Toronto clergyman (Congregationalist), will give a fair idea

[82] See report in *Globe* of January 10th, 1852.
[83] See report in *Globe* of January 13th, 1852.

of the stand taken by those who favoured rate bills upon parents. The first letter, published in the *Globe*, January 31st, 1852, is as follows:

> "I am happy to inform you that school section No. 1, Township of York, including the village of Yorkville, have this day negatived a proposal to have a free school, preferring to give the teacher £60 from the Public funds, and a right to charge 1s. 3d. per month for every child attending the school. The mechanics and labourers here have thus discharged the power, for there cannot be any such right, so wrongfully given them by the School Act, to educate their own children at the expense of their more wealthy neighbours. All praise to their honesty. Thus they will escape from the pauperizing tendencies of the free school system. They encourage their schoolmaster with the hope of being rewarded for making a good school. They suffer the proprietors of private schools to maintain a useful competition with the common school teacher; they keep up valuable select schools, and yet in return for the public fund, they will get free education for the children whose parents need exemption from the school fees.
>
> "May we not hope that the city of Toronto will next year follow this honourable example, and spurn the unrighteous counsel which is introducing communism in education to the undermining of property and society? The French people and the Normans ought to serve as warnings of the abyss to which this plausible socialism is enticing us."

The second letter was published in the Toronto *Globe*, February 5th, 1852:

> "The idea of the outlay for education being profitable for the holders of property, and thus justifying the impost, is much like a joke; for surely no one thinks it necessary to force upon men of property so great a gain, as they seldom need be convinced by their poor neighbours where their true interests lie. Gain indeed; why, probably three-fourths of the children now in the Toronto common schools will carry their education away to the West, and here be succeeded by others who will similarly want to use our property for their own benefit. Besides we might give free education to those who otherwise would be destitute of it, but make those purchase it who have the means.
>
> "While I thus dwell on the injustice of the arrangement, I do so because what is unjust cannot be wise, and not because the futility of the system is not otherwise apparent. The free system divests the teacher of all proprietary and personal interest in his school, and will speedily render him sycophantic and servile to his trustees, but haughty and negligent towards his pupils and friends. It will throw education into the hands of an electioneering party, and what kind of party that will be in such places as

> Toronto, need not be said. It will destroy all the confidence and love felt towards the teacher as the employee and friend of the child's parents, and substitute for them a cold respect due to the public official. It will render school attendance desultory and variable, because unpaid for, and always to be had for asking. Instead of the soft, familiar, and refined circle in which wise parents like to place their children, it will drive gentle youths and sensitive girls into the large herds of children with all the regimental strictness and coldness and coarseness by which such bodies must be marked, and thus, while the child asks bread you will give him a stone."

The opposition to free schools did not all come from wealthy property-owners who objected to educating the children of the poor. Voluntary schools, wholly independent of Government control and closely allied with some church, were already in operation in populous centres in Upper Canada. The managers of these schools had to depend wholly upon subscriptions and fees. So long as all schools were supported mainly from rate bills upon parents the purely voluntary schools were not at a serious disadvantage. But if free common schools were established, then all patrons of voluntary schools must submit to be taxed twice for the education of their children. The following from a *Globe* editorial of February 14th, 1852, shows that the effects of free schools upon voluntary schools were fully appreciated:

> "The *Patriot* of Tuesday gives us the real reason for his opposition to free schools. Formerly he talked of pauperizing the whole people, of socializing them, of a number of other direful evils to be dreaded as consequences of all free schools. In his last article, however, he admits that his main objection is, that denominational schools can never be supported beside those entirely free. We commend this fact to our friends who are sincerely opposed to sectarian education, and yet are not prepared to accept the principles of entire freedom. It is undoubtedly true what the *Patriot* says, denominational schools cannot exist beside free schools. So long as we continue to exact payment from parents, so long will efforts be made by the sects to obtain aid from the public funds and private support in order to weaken the common schools, draw away scholars from them, and destroy their efficiency. When the schools are supported entirely by taxation, no such attempts can be met with success. No sectarian school only partially supported by the State can compete with the free institution, and no one would be foolish enough to propose to endow more than one entirely free school. The people would not stand the taxation. The free principle is a deathblow to the attempts of the priests to get the education of the people into their own hands, to train up the children in classes and denominations, to shut them out from free knowledge, and to give them just what pleases their prejudiced

> views. The *Patriot* thinks it would be tyrannical to prevent the establishment of sectarian schools by means of a free system. We cannot see it in that light. The denominational plan has been tried in England, but it has failed. The schools were never established in sufficient numbers to educate the people. It is not reasonable to expect that sects managed by cliques of clergymen in the large towns should be able to manage a complete system of education for the people. The very idea is absurd. Are we then to give up our efforts for the education of the people, because these efforts would interfere with the small, ineffectual endeavours these denominations might make to secure proselytes to their churches through secular schools? Certainly not; the greatest friend to sectarian education could not admit that; and we who oppose that system rejoice that free schools, which are spreading so fast, will effectually put down the endeavours of the sects after educational influence which has produced both in Ireland and England such a scarcity of knowledge, and which have not been without their ill-effects in Canada."

These quotations will for us serve two purposes. They give a fair picture of the free school movement, and they sum up the arguments for and against State education. No thoughtful person in this age can observe the apathy of thousands of people in regard to the education of their children without at times feeling that these people would appreciate schools much more if they had to make some personal sacrifice to secure their advantages. But further thought is almost certain to convince us that free schools are the natural support of a democratic government, and that without their socializing influence a self-governing people would always be more or less at the mercy of demagogues.

CHAPTER VIII.

RYERSON AND SEPARATE SCHOOLS.

The purpose of this chapter is to set forth as briefly as possible the origin and development of Separate Schools in Upper Canada, showing incidentally the part taken in that development by Doctor Ryerson.

If we seek to discover the primary cause of our Separate School system we undoubtedly find it in the almost unanimous desire of the pioneer settlers to have the Common Schools established upon a basis of Christianity, and to secure for their children some positive instruction in the Holy Scriptures. From their standpoint secular schools were of necessity godless schools. We need also to remember that sectarian prejudices were more bitter seventy years ago than they are to-day. Dogma and religion were thought to be inseparable. To-day the various bodies of Christians throughout the world make much of what they hold in common; seventy years ago their grandfathers could not forget the petty differences of doctrine that held them apart. If the schools were to give religious instruction, and if the adoption of some form of instruction acceptable to all was impossible, then separate schools were the logical outcome. And as separate schools for each one of the many sects into which the scattered population of Upper Canada was divided were clearly impossible it naturally followed that such schools were established for Roman Catholics who were comparatively few in number, and who differed in doctrine from Protestants more radically than the various Protestant bodies differed amongst themselves. No one of the Protestant bodies could object to the reading of the Protestant Bible in the schools, but the Roman Catholics naturally objected to their children taking any part in such an exercise.

As pointed out in Chapter IV., the Common School Act of 1841 laid the foundation of Separate Schools. The provisions of that Act applied to the United Canadas. In any township or parish any number of dissentients might elect a trustee board and establish a school, receiving for its support public money in proportion to their numbers. It is clear that in practice under this clause a dissentient school could be established only where the dissentients were sufficiently numerous to furnish at least fifteen children of school age, and contribute a considerable sum for school purposes. Another clause in the Act of 1841 required the Governor to appoint, in towns and cities, school boards made up of an equal number of Protestants and Roman Catholics, the Protestants to manage schools attended by Protestant children and the Catholics to manage schools attended by Catholic children. But this clause made no provision for Roman Catholics from two or more city school sections combining to form one school for their children, and as Catholics in a single city section were seldom if ever numerous enough to form a school the Act was practically inoperative in securing separate Roman Catholic schools.

The Bill of 1841, as introduced into the Assembly, contained none of the above provisions for Separate Schools, and the question naturally arises, why were they inserted? Several petitions were presented from Boards of Education, and some from Synods of the Presbyterian Church, praying that the Bible be made a text-book in the schools. Bishop Strachan and the clergy of his diocese petitioned "that the education of the children of their own Church may be entrusted to their own pastors, and that an annual grant from the assessments may be awarded for their instruction."[84] The Roman Catholic Bishop of Kingston also petitioned against the Bill as brought in, but did not expressly ask for Separate Schools. It seems natural then to infer (and the Journals of the Assembly for 1841 bear out this inference), that the amendments granting Separate Schools were a compromise.

Another amendment authorized Christian Brothers to teach even if they were not naturalized British subjects. In 1843 the Act of 1841 was repealed in so far as it related to Upper Canada. The new Act made it unlawful in any common school to compel the child to read from any religious book or join in any religious exercise to which his parents or guardians objected. It also provided that if the teacher of a school were a Roman Catholic, then any ten householders or freeholders might petition for a Separate School with a Protestant teacher or, in the same way, Roman Catholics might form a Separate School if the teacher were a Protestant.

The grants to these Separate Schools were to be that proportion of the total school fund in any Municipal District that the children in actual attendance at the Separate School bore to the total number of children of school age in the district, and they were subject to the same rules and regulations regarding courses of study and inspection as the Common Schools.

In 1847 an amendment to the Common School Act was passed known as the Towns and Cities Act. This Act gave the Trustee Boards of towns and cities full power to determine the number of, and regulate, denominational schools. An extract from Ryerson's Annual Report for 1847 as presented to the Provincial Secretary will make clear the nature of the Act and the Chief Superintendent's views of it. Speaking of the provision for Separate Schools in the Act of 1843 he says:

> "I have never seen the necessity for such a provision in connection with any section of the Common School Law, which provides that no child shall be compelled to read any religious book or attend any religious exercise contrary to the wishes of his parents and guardians; and besides the apparent inexpediency of this provision of the law it has been seriously objected to as inequitable, permitting the Roman Catholics to have a denominational school, but not granting a similar right or privilege to any one Protestant denomination . . . nor does the Act of 1847 permit the election of any sectarian school trustees nor the appointment of a teacher of any religious persuasion as such even for a denomina-

[84] See copy in D. H. E., Vol. IV., p. 20.

> tional school. Every teacher of such school must be approved by the town or city school authorities. There are, therefore, guards and restrictions connected with the establishment of a denominational school in cities and towns under the new Act which did not previously exist; it, in fact, leaves the applications or pretensions of each religious persuasion to the judgment of those who provide the greater part of the local school fund and relieves the Government and Legislature from the influence of any such sectarian pressure. The effect of this Act has already been to lessen rather than to increase denominational schools, while it places all religious persuasions on the same legal footing, and leaves none of them any possible ground to attack the school law or oppose the school system. My Report on a system of Public Elementary Instruction for Upper Canada, as well as various decisions and opinions which I have given, amply show that I am far from advocating the establishment of denominational schools; but I was not prepared to condemn what had been unanimously sanctioned by two successive Parliaments."[85]

During the Legislative Session of 1850, and while the School Bill was under discussion, a petition was presented by prominent Roman Catholic authorities praying for some modifications of the provisions for Separate Schools in the Bill then before the House. The result was that the 19th clause of the Act of 1850 made it compulsory upon the Municipal Council of any township or the School Board of any city or town or incorporated village, upon the written request of twelve or more resident heads of families, to establish one or more Separate Schools for either Protestants or Roman Catholics. At this time only fifty-one Separate Schools were in operation in the whole of Upper Canada,[86] of which nearly one-half were Protestant.

According to a letter written by Ryerson to Hon. George Brown[87] there was a movement among certain Anglicans to secure Separate Schools for their children. Had Roman Catholics and Anglicans[88] both secured Separate Schools, it would have wrecked the Common School system, and these two denominations acting in concert were strong enough to defeat the Baldwin-Lafontaine Government. Acting on Ryerson's suggestion, the Government conceded in the main the Roman Catholic claim and secured their support to the Bill. This Bill gave Separate Schools one distinct advantage over the Act of 1843. It made their share of the Separate School fund that part of the total fund which the Separate School attendance bore to the total school attendance. But Separate School supporters were still far from hav-

---

[85] See copy in D. H. E., Vol. VII., p. 178.

[86] See circular, issued by Ryerson, of April 12th, 1850, to Municipal Councils on Act of 1850.

[87] See D. H. E., Vol. IX., p. 25.

[88] It is not meant to suggest that even a majority of the Anglicans would have done anything to wreck the Common School System. As a matter of fact, only a few of the Anglican laity sympathized with the extreme views of Bishop Strachan, either in Common School or University affairs.

ing their schools recognized as a right and placed on an equality with Common Schools. Separate Schools were granted as a privilege or concession, but not as a right. Let me quote from Ryerson's circular to town reeves on the Act of 1850: "But, notwithstanding the existence of this provision of the law since 1843, there were last year but 51 Separate Schools in all Upper Canada, nearly as many of them being Protestant as Roman Catholic; so that this provision of the law is of little consequence for good or for evil. . . . It is also to be observed that a Separate School is entitled to no aid beyond a certain portion of the School Fund for the salary of the teacher. The schoolhouse must be provided, furnished, warmed, books procured, etc., by the persons petitioning for the Separate School. Nor are the patrons or supporters of a Separate School exempted from any of the local assessments or rates for common school purposes."[89]

This makes it clear that Separate School supporters were liable to be taxed by the municipality for the support of Common Schools; they might be called upon to pay an assessment to build, repair or furnish a Common School, or to pay a part of the teacher's salary. On the other hand, the only aid they received in support of their own school was a share of the legislative and municipal grants which together made up the school fund.[90] It will at once be seen that every step toward free Common Schools placed the Separate School supporters at an increased disadvantage because it made them contribute more and more toward the Common School.

The Act of 1850 caused some friction in Toronto, where the Roman Catholics asked for a second Separate School. The Trustee Board refused on the ground that they were not legally compelled to establish more than one Separate School in the city and the Court of Queen's Bench upheld their decision. By the old Act, under which cities were divided into school sections, there was no legal bar to the establishment of a Separate School in every city school section. Ryerson thought the Roman Catholics had a grievance and consented to recommend the Bill giving a Separate School in each city ward or a Separate School for two or more wards united for such purpose. This amendment was passed in 1851 and caused considerable discussion. A large party in Upper Canada were opposed to Separate Schools on principle and objected to any legislation that would multiply them, make them more efficient and popular, or grant them more favourable financial support.

The attitude of the out-and-out opponents to Separate Schools was very well expressed by the following Bill,[91] introduced in 1851 by William Lyon Mackenzie:—

> "Whereas the establishment of sectarian or Separate Schools, upheld by periodical grants of money from a provincial treasury and placed under the control of the Executive Government through its Superintendents of Education and other civil officers, is a dangerous interference with the Common School system of

---

[89] See D. H. E., Vol. IX., p. 208.

[90] It was long a favourite argument of those opposed to Separate Schools that inasmuch as the bulk of the property was owned by Protestants, the Roman Catholics were not entitled to a share of the school fund reckoned on the basis of the pupils' attendance.

[91] See Journals of Canadian Assembly for 1851.

> Upper Canada, and if allowed to Protestants and Roman Catholics cannot reasonably be refused to Episcopalians, Presbyterians, Quakers, Tunkers, Baptists, Independents and other religious denominations; and whereas if it is just that any number of religious sects should have Separate Public Schools it is not less reasonable that they should have separate Grammar Schools, Colleges and professorships in the Universities; and whereas it is unjust for the State to tax Protestants in order to provide for the instruction of children in Roman Catholic doctrines or to tax Roman Catholics for religious instruction of youth in principles adverse to those of the Church of Rome; and as the early separation of children at school on account of the creeds of their parents or guardians would rear nurseries of strife and dissension and cause thousands to grow up in comparative ignorance who might under our Common School system obtain the advantages of a moral, intellectual and scientific education, be it enacted therefore that the nineteenth section of the Act of 1850 be repealed."

Mackenzie's Bill was defeated by 26 to 5. It lays down broad general principles that are not easy to overthrow, and no doubt several who voted against it would have been glad to see all young Canadians educated together. But if the right to have Separate Schools be granted, and it had been granted by successive School Acts for Upper Canada, then it seems naturally to follow that the Legislature was bound to place no obstacles in the way of their formation and to make them efficient.

Separate Schools were at first grudgingly granted as a privilege, but not as a right. Naturally, every extension of the privilege was used by the supporters of these schools as a vantage-ground from which to secure further privileges and gradually convert these into rights. At first the parties seceding from the Public Schools shared only in the school fund made up of the legislative grant and an equal sum levied by the district, town or city council—the whole being available only for the payment of teachers' salaries. Supporters of Separate Schools were liable to be taxed for the building and equipment of Public Schools in addition to the support of their own. They claimed a *pro rata* share of all moneys levied by taxation, and in some cases the law was invoked in an attempt to secure such share.

In 1853, a radical amendment was adopted by which Separate School supporters received a *pro rata* share of the legislative grant only, and upon subscribing for school purposes a sum equivalent to the grant secured were relieved of all taxation for Common School purposes. The Act of 1853 also gave the Separate School trustees power to issue certificates to the teachers employed by them, and the same power of levying rates upon the supporters of their schools as that exercised by trustees of Common Schools.

While the Separate School Bill of 1853 was before the Legislature, there was an attempt to introduce a clause establishing a general Board of Trustees for Separate or sectarian Schools in towns and cities. Ryerson went to Quebec to confer with the Attorney-General and vigorously opposed the Bill. His correspondence shows that he had no wish to place Separate Schools on an equality with Public Schools. In fact he wished to do nothing that would encourage or make easy their formation. The law as it stood allowed Separate Schools only when the teacher was of a different religious faith from those wishing the Separate School. A general Board of Separate School Trustees for every town or city would have greatly increased the number of Separate Schools. Ryerson says: "This is placing Sectarian Schools upon a totally different foundation from that on which they have always stood; it is the introduction of a system of sectarian schools without restriction and almost without conditions. . . . If there are city and town Boards of Sectarian School Trustees they will claim the right of appointing their own local superintendents, and thus their schools will be shut up against all inspection except that they themselves may please to require or permit. . . . Thus such a Board in Toronto might recognize and claim public aid for every child taught in convents and by other private teachers of the same religious persuasion. . . . If provision be made in each city and town to incorporate into one Board one religious persuasion, exempting it from the payment of school rates and authorizing it to tax and collect from its own members to any amount for school purposes, the application of any other religious persuasion in any such city or town cannot be consistently or fairly resisted. . . . The effect of all this would be to destroy the system of Public Schools in cities and towns and ultimately perhaps in villages and townships, and to leave all the poorer portion of the population and that portion of it connected with minor religious persuasions without any adequate and certain means of education. I think the safest and most defensible ground to take is a firm refusal to sanction any measure to provide by law increased facilities for the multiplication and perpetuation of sectarian schools."[92]

The attitude of the extreme opponents of Separate Schools may be made clear from the editorials of George Brown in the Toronto *Globe*. On April 2nd, 1853, he says:—

> "But under the new Bill the taxation of the Roman Catholic parents and the whole charge of the Separate Schools are to devolve on the Popish authorities. The schools are to become henceforth distinct, not only in their mode of tuition, but in the machinery by which they are to be conducted. They are to retain no vestige of connection with the general educational system, which is the pride and glory of the Canadian people. Any Roman Catholic has only to declare himself a supporter of a Separate School and straightway he is relieved from taxation for the maintenance of the general system. As at present constituted, there is a kind of guarantee that Roman Catholics are educated, that they are not left entirely in ignorance, but under Mr. Richards' Bill there would be none. . . . The plain and obvious intention of the Bill is the still further development of the sectarian element in our Common Schools. The Roman Catholics were not satisfied with what

[92] See D. H. E., Vol. X., pp. 172 and 173.

they had already gained. They wished to obtain their share of the annual Parliamentary grant, paid out of the revenue, which is made up almost exclusively from Protestant money. They wished to have their schools altogether free from the supervision of the general trustees. Their bishops went down to Quebec, the *Mirror* announcing their departure, and hinting at the object of their journey, and straightway we have the Bill from Mr. W. B. Richards, granting to them all they had demanded. If they had asked much more it would have been granted to them by the present Government. If this Bill passes into law, the sectarian system will be fully and thoroughly introduced, and must be carried out to its utmost extent. The Roman Catholics say that they are not satisfied to send their children to the Common Schools, and they are free from taxation. The Episcopalians are ready to say the same, and we ask whether in fairness we can refuse to one what we grant to the other? And then the Methodists will demand separate schools, and the Presbyterians, and all hopes of the education of the people may be abandoned. Yet this Bill has been introduced by a Government raised to power upon the principle that our school system should be free from clerical control. 'No sectarian schools' was the watchword at the last election among Reformers, yet one of the first measures introduced by the Reform Government is to establish sectarian schools more thoroughly than before. We look to them to abolish, and behold! they ratify and confirm the evils of their predecessors. Where is this to stop? When is the measure of the iniquity of this Government to be filled up?. . . Let our school system, the source of light and intelligence, be destroyed, and what remains to us of hope for the country? They, as it were, would go gradually back to the darkness of ignorance and superstition. We shall consider no institution safe from priestly encroachments if this Bill is carried. There is no point upon which the people of Upper Canada can be more severely wounded than their common schools. Every true patriot has fondly looked to them as the safeguards against the despotism of priestcraft, and against violence of an ignorant and, therefore, vicious populace. If they are sacrificed, if their noble endowment is scattered among the sects, frittered away on a dozen different school systems, if the priests are to take possession of all the avenues of knowledge, what will be the fate of this Province? Will it rise in the scale of nations, ever to be distinguished for the intelligence of its people, for its prosperity and advancement?"[93]

The following from the Toronto *Examiner*, reprinted in the *Globe* of April 7th, 1853, shows that the *Globe* was not alone in its opinions:—

"We are reluctantly forced to the conviction that the rupture,

[93] See bound volumes of *Globe* in Legislative Library, Toronto.

complete and final, of the Common School system of Canada is only a question of time. We were among those who looked anxiously to the Government for a liberal and decided policy on this momentous question. An examination of the supplementary School Bill which we give in other columns will bear us out but too fully, we fear, in pronouncing its liberality exceedingly questionable. . . . How different in Canada. Reformers have been bidding for Roman Catholic votes until they are likely to bid away every distinctive principle which they hold, and when this is done will it satisfy the ends of men whose mission is to establish in the place of free institutions the domination of priestcraft?"

The following from the Roman Catholic *Mirror*, quoted in the *Globe*, April 9th, 1853, shows that the Roman Catholics were well pleased with the Bill:

> "We freely admit that we had certain misgivings respecting the amount of relief which might be expected from the measure proposed, which from the haughty and dictatorial tone assumed by the Chief Superintendent of Schools for Upper Canada, in his late perambulations, we were prepared at least to regard with suspicion. The terms on which justice has been hitherto meted out in stinted and niggard instalments, under the existing law, and the many instances in which it has been withheld or contemptuously refused, may have rendered us over-sensitive; but we must acknowledge that when we observe Dr. Ryerson publicly promulgate the conditions on which he would concede to Catholics the privilege of directing the education of their own children, we were prepared to expect a reiterated legislative insult and a gross injustice, not a measure restrictive, partial and oppressive. We have been most agreeably disappointed; the Bill of the 'Honourable Attorney-General West,' with some slight modifications which can be readily introduced in committee, will form the basis of an educational system of sound principle, particularly calculated to do justice to all classes of the community."

The following resolutions of the Synod of the United Presbyterian Church, printed in the *Globe*, June 30th, 1853, shows the opinion of that body on the Common School question:—

> "Resolved. I. That this Synod approve of a national system of education, placing all the members of the community upon a level, and encouraging, as that now in force in this Province does, the use of the Scriptures under certain reasonable regulations, as are also prescribed therein.
>
> "II. Holding these views, we deeply regret to perceive the principle of sectarian schools, so distinctly recognized in the latest amendments of the Provincial School Act, and do strongly testify against such a principle as impolitic and mischievous, recogniz-

ing as it does the right of the Government to take the moneys of the public and appropriate them for the purpose of sustaining and extending religious distractions, and thereby continuing to stimulate the elements of discord throughout the community and mar greatly social interests.

"III. That this Synod recommend to those under their care the use of every proper and constitutional means to secure the repeal of all such statutes as recognize the principle of sectarian schools."

The movement for extended Separate School privileges was being championed by Bishop de Charbonnel, of Toronto. During 1852 he had a long controversy with Ryerson on the school question.[94] Ryerson's letters during this controversy make it quite clear that he thought Separate Schools a huge blunder, and that while he had honestly attempted to give Roman Catholics all the law allowed them he hoped and expected to see their schools die a natural death.

In his Report for 1852, the Superintendent points with pride to the fact that Separate Schools are not increasing. Indeed, he congratulates himself that the provision in the law allowing them is really a good thing, since it is not very effective in practice but yet acts as a safety valve to prevent violent opposition to the school system. He believed that the Roman Catholics themselves would ultimately see that a policy of isolation of their children would have the effect of cutting them off from many of their natural privileges as Canadian citizens. And had the Separate School Act of 1853 remained unaltered, events would likely have shown Ryerson to be correct in his views. He believed the Act of 1853 was final, and that without any municipal machinery for collecting their taxes Separate Schools would never become numerous.

In this he was greatly mistaken, as events proved. In 1854, the Roman Catholic Bishops of Toronto, Kingston and Bytown, drew up a Separate School Bill which they wished should become law. This Bill would have forced all Roman Catholics to support Catholic Separate Schools wherever such were established. It also had other provisions which Ryerson thought objectionable. In 1855 a Separate School Bill, known as the "Taché Bill," was introduced into the Legislative Council, and after some amendments adopted by both branches of Parliament. This Act differed from all previous Acts in that its provisions were exclusively for Roman Catholic Separate Schools. It repealed all previous legislation for Separate Schools in so far as Roman Catholics were concerned. It made possible the establishment of a Roman Catholic Separate School in any school section or any ward of a town or city on petition of ten Roman Catholic ratepayers and gave them a Separate School Board with their own Superintendent in towns and cities. Such Roman Catholic ratepayers were relieved from all municipal rates for Common School purposes, and received for their own school a *pro rata* share of the Legislative grant if they had an average attendance of 15 pupils. The Act also made possible general Boards of Separate School Trustees in towns and cities and gave all Separate School Boards power to license their own teachers and levy rates for Separate School purposes upon the supporters of those schools. The Act was in principle a distinct gain for

[94] See appendices to Journals of House of Assembly, 1852-1853.

the champions of Separate Schools, but it led to no rapid increase in the number of such schools. In 1858, only 94 Separate Schools were in existence with an enrolment of less than 10,000 children, as compared with an enrolment of 284,000 in the Public Schools. The Act of 1855 was really forced upon Upper Canada by the votes of members from Lower Canada, there being a majority of Upper Canada members against the Bill.

It would seem that the Roman Catholics did not gain by the Taché Bill as much as they expected. The following letter written to Dr. Ryerson from Quebec, on June 8th, 1855, by John (afterwards Sir John) A. Macdonald, Attorney-General for Upper Canada, who had charge of the Bill in the Assembly, shows that political exigencies played no small part in school legislation: "Our Separate School Bill, which, as you know, is now quite harmless, passed with the approbation of our friend, Bishop Charbonnel, who, before leaving here, formally thanked the administration for doing justice to his Church. He has got a new light since his return to Toronto, and he now says the Bill won't do. I need not point out to your suggestive mind that in any article written by you on the subject it is politic to press two points on the public attention: 1st, That the Bill will not, as you say, injuriously affect the Common School system. This for the people at large. 2nd, That the Bill is a substantial boon to the Roman Catholics. This to keep them in good humour. You see that if the Bishop makes the Roman Catholics believe that the Bill is no use to them there will be a renewal of an unwholesome agitation which I thought we had allayed."[95]

That Sir John A Macdonald was largely in agreement with Dr. Ryerson on the Separate School question is the opinion of Sir Joseph Pope, his biographer, who says on page 138 of his Memoirs: "Mr. Macdonald said that he was as desirous as anyone of seeing all children going together to the Common School, and if he could have his own way there would be no Separate School. But we should respect the opinions of others who differed from us, and they had a right to refuse such schools as they could not conscientiously approve of."

From 1855 to 1863, no important changes took place in the law governing Separate Schools. These schools were increasing very slowly, not so fast as the natural growth of the Roman Catholic population. In 1860, there were only 115 Separate Schools with an enrolment of 14,708 as compared with some 325,000 in the Public Schools. In 1860, Mr. (afterwards Honourable) R. W. Scott introduced a Bill planned to give Separate Schools additional privileges. Substantially the same Bill was introduced annually by Mr. Scott until 1863, when it passed with amendments, some of which were suggested by Dr. Ryerson. As a matter of fact, the Taché Act of 1855, which was suggested partly by the status of Protestant dissentient schools in Lower Canada, had imposed some useless but vexatious restrictions upon Separate School supporters. In 1862, Ryerson proposed to satisfy what he called the reasonable demands of Roman Catholics by making four changes, as follows:—[96]

1st. To allow the formation of Separate Schools in incorporated villages and in towns (the Taché Act allowed a Separate School only in the ward of a town and not

[95] See copy of letter in D. H. E., Vol. XII., p. 40.
[96] See D. H. E., Vol. XVII., pp. 192 and 193.

a school for the town as a whole); 2nd. To allow a union of two or more Separate Schools; 3rd. To make it unnecessary for a Separate School supporter annually to declare himself such; and 4th. To exempt Separate School trustees from making oath as to the correctness of their school returns.

The Scott Bill of 1863[97] as finally adopted by the Legislature, embodied all these provisions and some others of importance. Separate School teachers were to submit to the same examinations and receive the same certificates of qualification as Public School teachers, but all teachers qualified by law in Lower Canada were to be qualified teachers for Separate Schools in Upper Canada. This provision was to allow the teachers of religious orders[98] recognized by law as qualified in Lower Canada to teach in Separate Schools in Upper Canada. The Act also made taxpayers who withdrew their support from Separate Schools liable for their share of debts incurred while Separate School supporters in building or equipping Separate Schools. On the whole, the Scott Bill, while in its unamended form it aroused great opposition in Upper Canada, as finally adopted, tended to bring the Separate Schools into closer harmony with the principles governing Public Schools. The feature of the Bill that aroused most opposition was its being forced upon Upper Canada by votes of Lower Canadian members—there being a majority[99] of ten Upper Canada members against the third reading of the Bill in the Assembly. Such well-known men as John A. Macdonald, John Sandfield Macdonald and Wm. Macdougall supported the Bill, while George Brown, Alexander Mackenzie and Oliver Mowat opposed it.

Ryerson claimed[100] that he agreed to the amended Scott Bill only on the distinct understanding that it was to be a finality in Separate School legislation. He also claimed that the Roman Catholic Bishops of Quebec, Kingston and Toronto accepted the Bill as a final settlement. But nothing is final in legislation, and Dr. Ryerson ought to have known this. Legislation is as much the result of a process of evolution as any other institution of human society, and no three or four men, whether priests or laymen, could speak authoritatively and finally for the thousands of Roman Catholics in Upper Canada.

Separate Schools increased slowly. In 1863 they numbered 115, with 15,000 pupils, the Public Schools having during the same year 45,000 Roman Catholic pupils. In 1864, Separate Schools had increased to 147 with 17,365 pupils. In 1871, the number was 160, with 21,000 pupils.

Almost immediately after the Scott legislation of 1863, an agitation began for

[97] The Scott Bill, as originally introduced, made any Roman Catholic priest an ex-officio trustee of a Separate School in his parish; made all the property of a Separate School supporter exempt from taxation for Public School purposes, even though some of the property was outside a Separate School district; gave Separate School trustees unlimited power to form union sections; created a separate County Board of Examiners to license Separate School teachers, and gave the Superintendent of Education little or no power to control textbooks, holidays or inspection of Separate Schools.

[98] The Report of the Chief Superintendent for 1871 shows 70 teachers in Separate Schools belonging to religious orders out of a total of 249.

[99] See Journals of Canadian Assembly for 1863.

[100] See D. H. E., Vol. XVII., p. 219.

further amendments to the Separate School Act. Ryerson made strong objections partly on the ground of the alleged compact of 1863, and partly on the ground that no legislation could possibly make Separate Schools really popular and efficient outside of large towns and cities.

In 1865, the school administration was attacked by James O'Reilly, of Kingston, and, in a memorandum prepared as a reply to these attacks, Ryerson goes into some detail to justify his Separate School policy and reiterates his firm belief that sectarian schools must ever be relatively inefficient. He concludes as follows: "The fact is that the tendency of the public mind and of the institutions of Upper Canada is to confederation and not isolation, to united effort and not divisions. The efforts to establish and extend Separate Schools, although often energetic and made at great sacrifice, are a struggle against the instincts of Canadian society, against the necessities of a sparsely populated country, against the social and political interest of the parents and youth separated from their fellow-citizens. It is not the Separate School law that renders such efforts fitful, feeble and little successful; their paralysis is caused by a higher than human law, the law of circumstances—the law of nature, and the law of interest.

"If, therefore, the present Separate School law is not to be maintained as a final settlement of the question and if the Legislature finds it necessary to legislate on the Separate School question again, I pray that it will abolish the Separate School law altogether; and to this recommendation I am forced after having long used my best efforts to maintain and give the fullest effect and most liberal application to successive Separate School acts—and after twenty years' experience and superintendence of our Common School system."[101]

When the Confederation resolutions adopted at Quebec in 1864 were being discussed in the Canadian Assembly in 1865, an extended debate arose over the clause which secured for the minorities in Upper and Lower Canada the privilege of Separate Schools. Men like George Brown and Alexander Mackenzie, who had opposed the Scott Bill of 1863, defended the minority clause on the ground that it would place Upper Canada in no worse position than she already was in regard to sectarian schools, and that privileges given ought not to be withdrawn. The Assembly were almost unanimous in supporting the Separate School clause which was incorporated into the British North America Act.

No changes in Separate School legislation were made after Confederation until 1886, and the only events of passing importance in Separate School affairs were the objections raised in Kingston in 1865 and in Toronto in 1871 to visits of inspection by the Grammar School Inspector, who had been appointed to make these visits by the Council of Public Instruction. When Dr. Ryerson pointed out that these visits were authorized by the Scott Bill of 1863, the Bishops very gracefully waived their objections and the principle of Separate School inspection by Government officers was established. In 1874, the three High School Inspectors made a general inspection of Separate Schools. In their report to the Government they say: "The inspection of the Separate Schools derives an additional interest and importance from the peculiar position they occupy in our educational system. Among

[101] See copy of Memorandum, D. H. E., Vol. XVIII., pp. 304-316.

them we have found both well-equipped and ill-equipped, both well-taught and ill-taught schools. On the whole we regret that in the majority of cases the buildings, the equipment, and the teaching are alike inferior. There are but few Separate School teachers whose school surroundings are such as to make their positions enviable, and accordingly a large measure of approbation is due to those who have succeeded in doing good work. We have pleasure in stating that in many places the Separate School Boards are beginning to see that they must either make the schools under their charge more efficient or close them altogether. There are many things connected with the operation of the Separate School Act which invite comment; but we think it best to postpone the expression of our views until they are matured by the experience of another year."

Some years after this, in 1882, the Education Department adopted the plan of appointing special Roman Catholic Inspectors of Separate Schools. No doubt regular inspection of these schools has done much to increase their efficiency, but it is to be regretted that the plan of inspection adopted tends to widen still further the breach between them and the schools of the mass of the people.

Four years after Ryerson's death, the Act relating to Separate Schools was revised and amended. No new principles were introduced, but every amendment made tended to place Separate School supporters on an equality with supporters of Public Schools. The number of schools has gradually increased owing to the rapid increase in our urban population. In 1884 there were 207 Separate Schools, with 27,463 pupils; in 1894, 328 schools with 39,762 pupils; and in 1906, 443 schools with 50,000 pupils.

Perhaps the most important event connected with the history of Separate Schools since 1886 was the decision of the Judicial Committee of the Privy Council in November, 1906. This decision made it clear that the clause declaring persons qualified as teachers in Quebec at the time of Confederation to be qualified teachers of Separate Schools in Ontario applied only to individuals and not to religious corporations as such. The result will be that the Separate Schools ought soon to have a body of teachers with the same academic standing and the same normal training as the Public Schools.

CHAPTER IX.

RYERSON AND GRAMMAR SCHOOLS.

As already shown in the chapters on the early history of schools in Upper Canada, Grammar Schools were provided for before any provision was made for Common Schools. In fact the chief nominal purpose of the large grant of public land in 1799 was to endow Grammar Schools, and in 1807 schools were opened in each of the eight Districts into which Upper Canada was then divided. These schools were supposed to be classical schools, fashioned upon the model of the great English Public Schools. As a matter of fact they had no uniform standard of equipment, staff, course of study or graduation. A few schools, such as Cornwall, Kingston, York, and Niagara, were famous and turned out many able men. Some of the schools received pupils who could not read, and were in no sense secondary schools. As the population increased, new schools were opened. Although originally intended to be free schools, they all charged fees. The public grant, which was paid direct to the principal, was one hundred pounds for each school. As the population increased, new schools were opened, and by 1844, when Ryerson became Superintendent of Education, twenty-five Grammar Schools and Academies were in operation.

These schools were managed by trustees appointed by the Crown, but were under no proper Government control. They were never really inspected. Each school was a law unto itself. All were supposed to teach Latin and Greek, but in many of them there was not a single pupil studying either of these languages. They were handicapped in many ways. For years there were no good elementary schools from which they could draw pupils with a foundation for a secondary education. During the same long period there were in Upper Canada no colleges to which graduates of Grammar Schools might go for professional training. This gave these schools a wide scope and great opportunities, but few seized the opportunities. The poverty of the people and the natural apathy of many in regard to education also prevented the development of good schools.

Good schools are possible only with good teachers, and good teachers in Upper Canada were not easily secured. The professions of law and medicine then, as now, were much more attractive than teaching for men of ability and education. Mercantile life also offered great opportunities. The result was that the Grammar Schools were often in charge of incompetent teachers.

Ryerson's commission gave him no control over Grammar Schools. But his first Report in 1846 recommended a graded, unified system of schools from the

Common School to the University. He also pointed out that these Grammar Schools which were intended for a special work were teaching everything taught in a Common School. In his Report for 1849 he recommended a commission of inquiry into the state of Grammar Schools and showed that the whole thirty or forty schools had matriculated only eight students into the University during that year. He suggested a fixed course of studies, a minimum qualification for entrance, and Government inspection. "Surely," he says, "it never could have been intended that the Grammar Schools should occupy the same ground as Common Schools, should compete with them, thus lowering the character and efficiency of both. . . . I am far from intimating an opinion that there are no efficient Grammar Schools in the Province, even under the present system or rather absence of all system. There are several instances in which separate apartments for different classes of pupils are provided and assistance employed to teach the English branches, but such examples are rather exceptions to the general rule than the rule itself. The general rule is whether there be an assistant or not to admit pupils of both sexes and all ages and attainments for A B C and upwards into schools which ought to occupy a position distinct from and superior to that of the Common Schools. Equally far be it from me to intimate that there is any deficiency of qualifications on the part of masters of Grammar Schools. But I doubt not that they will be the first to feel how much the efficiency and pleasures of their duties will be advanced by the introduction of a proper and uniform system as they will be the first to confess, '*non omnia possumus omnes*.'"[102]

After the Common Schools had been brought under the rule of law it was inevitable that the Grammar Schools should be reorganized. In 1850, Francis Hincks introduced a Grammar School Bill prepared by Doctor Ryerson. This Bill aimed at bringing the schools under popular control and administering them on lines similar to those governing Common Schools. Trustees were to be appointed by County Councils; Trustee Boards were to have power to levy rates for buildings, equipment and apparatus; the Legislative grant was to be distributed to the several Districts on the basis of population, but only when local contributions made up a sum equal to the grant exclusive of pupils' fees; the programme of studies was to be broad enough to prepare for matriculation; the Council of Public Instruction was to fix Grammar School programmes, prescribe texts and appoint inspectors. A meteorological station was to be established in connection with one Grammar School in each District. This Bill was withdrawn, but a similar one[103] became law on January 1st, 1854. The new Act, as amended in 1855, also provided for uniting Grammar Schools with Common Schools and provided that a Grammar School master, unless a university graduate, must secure a certificate from a Board of Examiners appointed by the Council of Public Instruction. This Act also authorized an annual appropriation of £1,000 to establish a Model Grammar School in connection with the Normal School, authorized the Council of Public Instruction to appoint Grammar School inspectors, and made up a liberal grant to secure librar-

[102] See extract from Report of 1849, published in D.H.E., Vol. VIII., p. 291.

[103] This Act did not give trustees power to levy assessments, but they might ask municipal councils to do so. The distribution of the Legislative grant did not, as in the Bill of 1850, depend upon the raising of any fixed amount by the local Board.

ies and apparatus. After this legislation, the Council of Public Instruction drew up regulations governing the curriculum of Grammar Schools and took steps to bring about the use of uniform texts. From the first there were two courses of study, a general English course and a classical course leading to matriculation. The head master of each Grammar School was required to conduct an examination of candidates for admission, the requirements being intelligible reading from any common reading book, spelling, writing, elementary arithmetic, and the elements of English grammar, with definitions of geography.

In the autumn of 1855, the Grammar Schools were inspected, those in the east by Thomas Jaffray Robertson and those in the west by William Ormiston. Their reports show that many of these schools were indifferent and a few hopeless. Perhaps half of them were doing fairly well. The attendance averaged about thirty, of whom nearly one-half were studying Latin. Half of the schools admitted female pupils. The highest salary paid a head master was $1,200, while the average for head masters was $700. Few of the schools had two masters. Half the total number of head masters were graduates of British or Canadian universities. In some cases the teachers were paid a fixed salary, and in some cases they got the Government grant and the school fees. These fees averaged about three dollars per quarter. In a few cases the head master had a dwelling in connection with the school.

The inspectors criticised the buildings, equipment and grounds severely, as the following extracts will show:—

> "Of the Grammar School houses seventeen were originally built for school purposes and several of them, which were spacious and substantial buildings, may be classed as good; ten were somewhat inferior; and one, a very old wooden building, could scarcely be considered habitable. Nine schools were carried on in premises rented for the purpose and were in most instances totally unfit. In many cases the grounds attached to the schoolhouses were partially or entirely unfenced, and the sheds or outhouses were in a shameful state of neglect. Even in the neatest premises I saw no attempt at ornament; not a tree, shrub or flower to awaken or cultivate a taste so simple and natural in itself and so easily gratified as it could be in rural districts. . . . Very many of these houses are inferior to the Common Schools. In most cases the premises present a dull, unthrifty and unattractive appearance, destitute alike of ornament and convenience, without fence, shed, well, tree, shrub or flower, while within an entire lack of maps, charts and apparatus is with too few exceptions the general rule."[104]

Two years later the same inspectors made another general report on Grammar Schools. They found some improvements but many weak schools doing the most elementary Common School work. They deprecated the practice, then becoming somewhat common, of establishing new Grammar Schools in small villages.

---

[104] See copy of Report in D. H. E., Vol. XII., p. 81.

It is abundantly clear from Ryerson's Reports, 1856-58, that he was dissatisfied with the progress being made in Grammar Schools and eager to attempt their improvement by means of further legislation. The most serious problem was that of providing an adequate and certain financial support for these schools. The schools were managed by trustee boards appointed by County Councils, but were attended largely by pupils of towns and cities. The people using them and contributing largely to their support were not given the power to manage them.

Ryerson was also very doubtful about the result of the experiment authorized in 1854, of uniting Common and Grammar Schools. The union gave trustee boards increased freedom of management, but in many cases the union school became, for all practical purposes, a common school, having, perhaps, three or four senior pupils studying Latin and Greek. Such schools brought all Grammar Schools into contempt.

The report of the Grammar School inspector on the schools of Eastern Ontario, for 1860, shows that things were far from satisfactory:

> "With the exception of two or three really good schools our Grammar Schools in the extreme East are in a very low state. Some of them I can only designate as infant schools. Nor do I see anything from the localities in which they are placed or the present state of the Grammar School law which gives me any hope of amelioration. Advancing civilization and the material growth of the country in time may act upon them, but immediate remedies and those of a stringent nature are imperatively needed. . . . The want of a class of specially trained Grammar School masters who have taken this as a permanent profession for life is a great drawback to the efficiency of our schools. The supposed inferior social status of the Grammar School master and the larger rewards held out for superior mental activity in the other professions turn aside most of those who are most eminently qualified for the scholastic office. Of the twenty-two schools mentioned in my report six were in the hands of persons who avowedly were making teaching the stepping-stone to the attainment of other professions, as law, medicine, or the church. Several were evidently conducted by persons who had taken to teaching after having failed in other walks of life. Comparatively few were held by those who were fitted for their office by previous training, or were devoting themselves entirely to their work as the main business of their lives."[105]

There seems also to have been a disposition to unduly multiply Grammar Schools because they were supported so largely by the Legislative grant. The Rev. Dr. Paxton Young, Inspector of Grammar Schools, in his report for 1864, says: "The too free and inconsiderate exercise by County Councils of the large power thus entrusted to them has led to a heedless and most unfortunate multiplication of the Grammar Schools, and the evil instead of showing any symptoms of abatement appears to be growing worse from year to year. In 1858 the number of the schools

[105] See D. H. E., Vol. XVI., pp. 148, 149.

was seventy-five; in 1860 it was eighty-eight; in 1863 it had risen to ninety-five; and the number of recognized schools is now as high as one hundred and eight. Not a few of the schools thus hastily established are Grammar Schools in name rather than in reality, the work done in them being almost altogether Common School work, which, as a rule, would be much better performed in a well-appointed Common School. I believe that County Councils are often led to establish Grammar Schools in localities where they are not needed under the idea that if the schools should be productive of no good at any rate they can do no harm. There could not be a greater mistake. Men ought to be wise enough by this time to understand that all public institutions, especially if forming parts of a great plan, must, where unnecessary, be positively bad. Needless and contemptible Grammar Schools are a blot upon the whole school system, the sight of which is fitted to shake the confidence of the country in the administrative wisdom or firmness of those to whom the direction of educational matters is committed. When it is considered that the apportionment from the Grammar School fund to a particular county is divided according to certain fixed principles between the different schools in that county, it will be seen that the disposition manifested by some councils to secure the largest number of schools for their county, is practically a disposition to secure quantity for quality, for as the number of schools is augmented the salaries of the masters are diminished, the tendency of which is, of course, to throw the schools into the hands of a lower grade of teachers. . . . About three out of every five Grammar Schools in Upper Canada have Common Schools united with them, and, in not a few instances, where unions have not yet been formed, I found a strong disposition existing to enter into such an arrangement. I made it my business to inquire particularly into the benefits supposed to result from the union of the Common with the Grammar Schools. The chief advantage was in almost every case admitted to be a pecuniary one. By the existing law Grammar School trustees have of themselves no power to raise money for Grammar School purposes, but in case of the Common and Grammar Schools becoming united the joint boards may levy money for the support of the united schools. This being so, it is easy to comprehend how strongly the trustees of a Grammar School who feel their hands tied up from doing anything to put the school in an efficient state may be tempted to make with the Common School Board a league which will give them a voice in the important matter of taxation. . . . But of nothing am I more convinced than that as a rule such a union is undesirable. In a large number of instances it throws upon the Grammar School master the necessity of receiving into his room, and personally instructing, Common School pupils, as well as those whom it is his more particular duty to attend to. A consequence of this is that he cannot afford the Grammar School pupils the time that is necessary for drilling them in the subjects that they are studying."[106]

But Doctor Young saw much promise in the schools, as the following from the same Report will show: "Leaving out of view schools of this sort, I do not hesitate to say that the Grammar Schools of Upper Canada are, as a class, not only in the promise of what they may become, but in what they actually are at the present

[106] See copy of Report in D. H. E., Vol. XVIII., pp. 199-205.

moment, an honour to the country. We must not look for too much. It would be preposterous to expect at this early period in the history of our Province, that its Grammar Schools generally should be able to bear comparison with the better classical and mathematical schools of Great Britain and Ireland. To this Canada does not pretend, but she has begun well, and appears to be steadily, if not rapidly, progressing."

In June, 1865, Ryerson went to Quebec to press upon the Government the necessity of a new Grammar School bill. As the Confederation scheme was approaching maturity he found the Government unwilling to embark upon any legislation that might prevent an early prorogation. Mr. John A. Macdonald suggested that the difficulty might be met by a regulation issued under the authority of the Council of Public Instruction. This was accordingly done, and the Council immediately framed regulations as follows: First, the Legislative grant was to be apportioned on the basis of the attendance of those learning Greek and Latin, as certified by the Grammar School Inspector. Second, no school was to receive any portion of the Legislative grant unless suitable accommodations were provided, and unless there were an average of at least ten pupils learning Latin and Greek, nor were any pupils to be admitted or continued in a Grammar School unless they were learning Latin and Greek.

This absurd regulation never went into effect, as the Legislature passed a Grammar School Bill in the latter part of 1865. The new Bill made each city a county for Grammar School purposes; it allowed County Councils to appoint half the Grammar School trustees, the other half being appointed by the village or town council where the school was situated. This latter provision was planned to give increased local control and thus create a stronger interest in the management of the schools. The distinction which had so long existed between senior and junior county Grammar Schools[107] was abolished and the Legislative grant was apportioned solely on the basis of attendance, but no school was to share the grant unless there was raised from local sources, exclusive of pupils' fees, a sum equal to half the grant. It was made more difficult to establish new schools. Only graduates of universities in British dominions were to be eligible for head masters' positions. On the suggestion of the Hon. William Macdougall, a clause was inserted providing for a grant of fifty dollars a year to those Grammar Schools giving a course of elementary military instruction.

The Report of Rev. Geo. Paxton Young on the Grammar Schools in 1865 is of great interest, read in the light of nearly half a century's progress in the higher education of women. I shall quote his exact words:

> "I have frequently been asked whether I considered it desirable that girls should study Latin in the Grammar Schools. It is, in my opinion, most undesirable; and I am at a loss to comprehend how any intelligent person acquainted with the state of things in our Grammar Schools can come to a different conclusion. . . . Since I became Inspector, I have not met with half a dozen girls

[107] This senior Grammar School, being the one first established in each county, had drawn a larger Legislative grant than the others.

in the Grammar Schools of Canada by whom the study of Latin has been pursued far enough for the taste to be in the least degree influenced by what has been read. Aesthetically, the benefits of Grammar Schools to girls are *nil*. . . . It may perhaps be said that although they have for the most part made but little progress in Latin up to the present time, a fair proportion of them may be expected to pursue the study to a point where its advantages can be reaped. I do not believe that three out of a hundred will. As a class, they have dipped the soles of their feet in the water, with no intention or likelihood of wading deeper into it. They are not studying Latin with any definite object. They have taken it up under pressure at the solicitation of the teachers or trustees to enable the schools to maintain the requisite average attendance of ten classical pupils or to increase that part of the income of the schools which is derived from public sources. In a short time they will leave school to enter on the practical work of life without having either desired or obtained more than the merest smattering of Latin, and their places will be taken by another band of girls who will go through the same routine. It may perhaps be urged that these remarks are as applicable to as large a number of the Grammar School boys as they are to the girls. I admit that they are; and I draw the conclusion that such boys, equally with the girls in the Grammar Schools, are wasting their time in keeping up the appearance of learning Latin. It would be unspeakably better to commit them to first-class Common School teachers, under whose guidance they might have their reflective and aesthetic faculties cultivated through the study of English and of those branches which are associated with English in good Common Schools. This would, of course, diminish the number of the Grammar Schools in the Province; but it might not be a very grievous calamity, especially if it led to the establishment of first-class Common Schools in localities where inferior teachers are now employed."[108]

It was a part of a Grammar School inspector's duty to examine the pupils who had been admitted by the Grammar School masters and reject any who were too immature or were insufficiently prepared. Dr. Young complains strongly in his Report of 1865 of the poor teaching of English grammar. In some cases he had to reject more than half those admitted. He found pupils wholly unable to parse such easy sentences as: "The mother loved her daughter dearly," "John ran to school very quickly," "She knew her lesson remarkably well."

It is doubtful whether the Grammar School Bill of 1865 made any real improvement in the schools. Without denying that some of them were doing a good work, and that as a force in the national life they were fostering some love for higher education, it is safe to assert that they were not very closely related to the real needs of the people. Their aim was narrow. Their very name shows this. There

[108] See copy of Report in D. H. E., Vol. XIX., pp. 96, 97.

was a crying need in the country for schools that would give an advanced English and scientific education with classic and modern languages to those who wished to pursue university studies. But the most of the Grammar Schools aimed only at a study of Latin and Greek, and indeed the Grammar School legislation and the regulations of the Council of Public Instruction had made a certain number of Latin pupils one of the conditions upon which a Grammar School might receive a public grant.

The Act of 1865 soon showed some disastrous tendencies. It did not check the desire to form unions between Grammar Schools and Common Schools, as such unions made it easier to levy a rate in support of the union schools, and thus comply with the conditions upon which Grammar Schools received grants. The clause in the new Act making average attendance the basis of attendance, together with a regulation of the Council of Public Instruction which counted only Latin pupils in making the grant, led the head masters of union schools to draft every available pupil into the Grammar School departments[109] and put them all, boys and girls, into Latin. Often they were not prepared for such work and got no real benefit from it. They wasted their time and lost the benefits of a sound English education which a good Common School would have given them. Hundreds of boys and girls who had no foundation for a classical education, and who had no prospect of ever advancing far enough to receive any solid knowledge of Latin, were making a pretence of studying it in order that the school might draw a Government grant. Ignorant parents raised no objections, thinking perhaps that Latin possessed some charm which would be an "open sesame" for the future advancement of the boys and girls.

Dr. Ryerson was not the man to diagnose the case. But the hour brought forth the man, and that man was George Paxton Young, one of the Inspectors of Grammar Schools. In two very able Reports[110] presented in 1867 and 1868, he sets forth clearly and convincingly the defects of the system then in operation and suggests the direction that reforms should take to make the Grammar Schools serve a useful purpose. He wished to see their character wholly changed. He did not undervalue classics, but he believed that a smattering of classics was of no benefit, and that it caused a waste of time that might be given to subjects of real value. He wished to see High Schools that would give an advanced English training, together with natural science, mathematics, and history. He did not believe in forcing all to study Latin, nor did he believe in apportioning grants to High Schools on the basis of the number of pupils studying Latin. He wished to see better Common Schools and objected to the plan of union which robbed the Common School of its older pupils and degraded its function. Speaking of this, he says: "The number of union schools is increasing and is likely to increase. In many of the schools of this class all the Common School pupils, boys and girls alike, who have obtained a smattering of English grammar are systematically drafted into the Grammar School. The

[109] It should be remembered that while a Public School pupil drew less than one dollar per year Legislative grant, the moment this pupil was enrolled in a Grammar School he drew from $20 to $35 yearly. In 1872, the average Legislative grant to a Public School pupil was 40 cents, and to a Grammar School pupil $20. See D. H. E., Vol. XXIV., p. 302.

[110] See copy of Report in D. H. E., Vol. XX., pp. 98-128.

consequence is that in localities where such a system is followed there is no mere Common School education (observe I say mere Common School education) given to any pupils, boys or girls, which is not of the most elementary description; and not only have the Grammar Schools thus become to a great extent girls' schools as well as boys' schools, but—what is especially noteworthy—the girls admitted to these schools are in a majority of instances put into Latin as a matter of course; in other words, the study of Latin is made practically a condition of their admission into the Grammar School. Will any man say that this state of things is satisfactory, a state of things in which the Common Schools are degraded by being suspended from the exercise of all their higher functions? Unless I misunderstand the object of the Common School law, the Common Schools are designed to furnish a good English and general education to those desiring it. But how can this end be accomplished where the Common Schools are subject to arrangements under which the highest stage of advancement ever reached by the pupils is to be able to parse an easy English sentence? . . . Children under thirteen years of age who do not mean to take a classical course of study have no educational wants which the Common Schools, properly conducted, are not fitted to supply. For children of thirteen and upwards who have already obtained such an education as may be got in good Common Schools, it would, I think, be well to establish English High Schools—a designation which I borrow from the United States although, unfortunately, I have only a very vague idea of what the High Schools in the United States are."

Dr. Young strongly urged a more rigid inspection of Grammar Schools and the apportioning of the Legislative grant upon the basis of Inspectors' reports. As so many girls had been drafted into Grammar Schools and put in grammar classes apparently to increase the school grant, it was proposed during 1868 to allow only fifty per cent. of girls' attendance to count in apportioning the grant and even to make no allowance whatever for attendance of female pupils in future years. This opened up the whole question of co-education of the sexes in Grammar Schools and caused lively debates in the Legislature and in Teachers' Institutes. The general opinion seemed to prevail that girls should have equal rights with boys but that the law should be so amended as to remove all pressure upon girls to study Latin.

After one or two abortive attempts, a Bill reorganizing Grammar Schools was passed in 1871. This Bill abolished the term "Grammar School," and substituted that of "High School." Adequate provision was to be made in each High School for an advanced English education, including natural sciences and commercial subjects. The study of Latin, Greek and modern languages was to be at the option of the pupils' parents or guardians. Provision was made for a superior class of High School, to be known as Collegiate Institutes. These schools were required to have at least four masters and an average of not less than sixty boys studying Latin or Greek, and were to receive a special grant of $750 a year. County Councils were empowered to form High School districts and provision was made by which the High School Board could levy an assessment upon the district. High School vacations were extended from July 1st to August 15th. A very important feature of the new Bill was the provision for the admission of pupils. The county, city or town Inspector of Schools, the Chairman of the High School Board and the head master of the High School were constituted a Board with power to conduct a written examination and admit pupils according to regulations prescribed by the Council of Public Instruction.

At first the local examining Board set the entrance papers, but this plan was soon superseded by one requiring uniform papers set by the High School Inspectors. This aroused a storm of opposition, and the resolution of the Council of Public Instruction requiring uniform papers was set aside by an Order-in-Council. But the plan of uniform papers was so sensible, and so much chaos resulted from the other plan, that by 1874 the Government authorized a uniform entrance examination which shut out immature pupils and those insufficiently prepared. It raised the status of High Schools, enabling them to begin advanced work, and indirectly increased the efficiency of the Public Schools by fixing a standard of attainment. The Legislature also made further provision for High Schools by appropriating an additional $20,000 a year, exclusive of the grants to be given to Collegiate Institutes.

The Act of 1871 provided for a minimum Legislative grant[111] for each High School, and made the maximum grant depend upon average attendance. The Rev. George Paxton Young had, in his last Report as Grammar School Inspector, strongly recommended the adoption in a modified form of the English system of payment by results. He wished to see the High Schools graded by the Inspectors according to their general efficiency and the grant based upon this grading. In 1872 the High School Inspectors, Messrs. McKenzie and McLellan, urged the adoption of a similar plan and showed how it would serve as a stimulus to better work in all the schools. They also pointed out how such a plan would encourage Boards to employ good teachers, since they would have a pecuniary interest in keeping up a good school.

The Act of 1871 gave the Council of Public Instruction a large measure of control over textbooks to be used in High Schools. The Council issued lists of those authorized, and this did much to bring about uniformity in courses of study. Previous to 1871, many High Schools had only one teacher, but the new legislation required at least two for High Schools and four for Collegiate Institutes. To secure this required much firmness on the part of Dr. Ryerson. Even two teachers were wholly unable to do efficient work in large High Schools, and there was no easy way to force School Boards to employ more. The Superintendent had steadily to oppose a tendency to form weak High Schools, and in some cases Grammar Schools which had been able to exist in a sickly state under the old law were wholly unable to meet the requirements of the Act of 1871, which threw some of the burden of support upon the local municipality.

The Inspectors' Reports for 1874 emphasize the need of additional teachers, the poor quality of work done in English literature, and the necessity of increased provision for natural science. Referring to the latter, the Inspectors' joint Report speaks as follows: "In regard to the direct utility of the knowledge imparted, the

[111] The minimum grant per school was $400. The High Schools of the Province had, in 1872, from Legislative grant and County Councils, $105,000. This was more than $1,000 per school and about $30 per pupil. Many of the High Schools charged no fees.

physical sciences are equalled by few subjects of study We regret to report that the teaching of science is not making progress in the schools. For this there are many reasons, of which perhaps the most important are the lack of apparatus and the impracticable character of the prescribed programme of studies. All places might advantageously follow the example of Whitby and fit up a science room, that is, a room to be devoted to the teaching of science and furnished with the necessary appliances and apparatus. It cannot too often be inculcated that there can be no effective teaching of chemistry without experiments. Effective teaching implies first of all a qualified teacher, and few of our masters consider themselves well qualified to teach any of the physical sciences. Yet the number of masters qualified to teach in this Department is increasing every year and it is much to be regretted that where the master is qualified he is often compelled, if he wishes to teach chemistry, to provide the apparatus at his own expense. The public indifference to the claims of physical science is greater than the indifference of the masters. Besides, three-fourths of High School Boards either are so poor, or believe themselves to be so poor, that they will grumble if asked to spend $10.00 annually for chemical purposes."[112]

Progress on the whole was rapid. Several weak schools were closed,[113] but they were schools which should never have been opened. Fees were either abolished or lowered.[114] The standard for pupils' admission was gradually raised and the old "Grammar Schools" were truly doing the work for which they were established in 1807.

Much was yet to be desired in the qualifications of High School masters. In 1874, one hundred out of one hundred and six head masters were university graduates, but forty-five assistants held only Second Class Normal School Certificates, or County Certificates, and twenty-three schools had to employ teachers for a whole or a part of the year without any legal qualifications. The average salary of head masters was $930.00, of male assistants $664.00, and of female assistants $416.00. The following extract from the Inspector's Report is interesting in the light of what has since been accomplished: "In the absence of any special training college or chair of pedagogy in the University, we would suggest that as so many men are pursuing a collegiate course, with a view to becoming High School masters, it would be well for the Government to establish a lectureship in Education. It would not, we think, be difficult if proper encouragement were given to secure the services of several experienced and skilled educationists, one of whom might deliver a short course of lectures on the above subjects during each college session."

Perhaps no part of our school system has developed more since Ryerson retired in 1876 than our High Schools. But this development has been almost wholly a natural growth. True, there has been much legislation and many changes in departmental regulations, but nothing of a revolutionary character. The opening of the doors of the universities to women and their increased employment as teach-

[112] See copy of Report in D. H. E., Vol. XXV., pp. 244-245.

[113] About fifteen in all.

[114] Out of 106 schools in operation in 1875, no less than 81 were absolutely free. Fees in the others varied from 75 cents to $6.00 per quarter, the average being $2.70.

ers has led to their being placed on an absolute equality with men in the High Schools and in all graduating examinations. The number of schools has almost doubled and the teaching of every department has been improved; incompetent teachers have given place to those having high academic and professional training; natural science has been greatly strengthened and the teaching of languages much improved; good laboratories have been built; spacious buildings with fine grounds have become the rule; the number of students preparing for university matriculation has multiplied many times; the average salaries of teachers have more than doubled, and finally the High Schools are so adapting themselves to the social needs of the people that they are becoming as much the schools of the people as are the Public Schools.

CHAPTER X.

RYERSON AND THE TRAINING OF TEACHERS.

Normal Schools were mooted in Upper Canada before Ryerson became Superintendent. As early as 1843, Sir Francis Hincks said that the school system would never be complete without them.[115] In his Report on a System of Education made in 1846, Ryerson made it clear that any system of education must have as its basis trained teachers, and to secure trained teachers was almost impossible without Normal Schools. His report gives details of the Normal School systems of Great Britain and Ireland, France, Holland, Germany, and the United States. One or two schools had just been established in Massachusetts and one in Albany. Ryerson visited these, but was most favourably impressed with the Dublin Normal and Model Schools, as managed by the Commissioners of the Irish National Board of Education, and our first Normal School was modelled largely after the Dublin type.

The legislation of 1846 appropriated £1,500 for fitting up a Normal School building and made an additional appropriation of £1,500 per annum for maintenance. The School Bill of 1846 created a Council of Public Instruction to work with the Chief Superintendent, and placed the proposed Normal School under its management. The Council of Public Instruction lost no time in beginning work. As early as May, 1846, they were planning an early opening of the Normal School, and were in communication with John Rintoul, of the Dublin Normal School, about accepting the head mastership of the proposed Normal School at Toronto. It was proposed to give Mr. Rintoul £350, Halifax currency, and £100 for moving expenses. Mr. Rintoul accepted the appointment, resigned his position in Dublin, and was about to leave for Canada when, owing to some domestic affliction, he had to abandon his plans. The Commissioners of the Irish National Board then selected Thomas Jaffray Robertson to take Rintoul's place and the Council of Public Instruction chose as his assistant Mr. Henry Hind, of Thorne Hill. Robertson sailed from Ireland in July, 1847, and in November of the same year the Normal School was opened.

It was a part of Ryerson's plan that the several District Councils of Upper Canada should choose two or three promising young men and send them to the Normal School, paying at least part of their expenses. The following extract from the Regulations issued by the Council of Public Instruction in 1847 will illustrate the requirements for admission to the first Normal School in Upper Canada: "1st. That the Provincial Normal School shall be open about the 1st of July next, and the first

[115] See extract from his speech, Chap. IV., pp. 101, 102.

session shall continue until the middle of October, 1847. 2nd. That every candidate for admission into the Normal School, in order to his being received, must comply with the following conditions: He must be at least sixteen years of age; produce a certificate of good moral character signed by a clergyman; be able to read and write intelligibly and be acquainted with the simple rules of arithmetic; must declare in writing that he intends to devote himself to teaching (other students not candidates for school teaching to be admitted only on paying fees and dues to be prescribed). 3rd. Upon the foregoing conditions candidates for school teaching shall be admitted to all the advantages of the Normal School without any charge either for tuition or for books. 4th. Candidates shall lodge and board in the city under such regulations as shall from time to time be approved by this Board."[116]

The school was formally opened by Dr. Ryerson, November 1st, in the presence of a distinguished company. The Model School was opened the following February.

The Normal School pupils were, many of them, poorly equipped for a course of training. They had received no adequate secondary education. In fact, many of them were direct from the Common Schools. A few were mature men who had a considerable teaching experience.[117]

It was necessary to give a broad academic course and judiciously interweave some professional training. Grammar and mathematics received much greater attention than their importance merited. Physical science and natural philosophy, together with some agricultural chemistry, received a prominent place on the programme. Geography was also made much of, but it was largely mathematical and political and elaborately illustrated with globes and maps. Literature and history were taught, but not in a way to arouse much enthusiasm. Pupils were supposed not to learn by heart what they did not understand, but there was in practice much memory work and repetition of rules.

On the whole, the Normal School was approved by all classes of people, and the teachers trained there were in great demand. But there was some criticism, especially of the provision by which four shillings a week was granted to students to aid them in paying their board. Inasmuch as this money was deducted from the school grant, it was argued that the teachers in service were actually educating in the Normal School others who would displace them. Exception was also taken to granting aid to students who had no intention of making teaching their life work. To meet this difficulty, students accepting public money towards their expenses were required to give assurance that they would teach a stated time, and others, called private pupils, were charged fees for tuition.

In 1849 the experiment was made of a nine months' session, but the country was not yet ready for this step and the attendance was so reduced that the plan was abandoned.

In 1850, the Council of Public Instruction attempted to widen the influence of the Normal School by sending the Normal School masters to attend Teachers'

[116] See Report of Superintendent of Education for 1848.

[117] Women were not admitted until the opening of the second term in 1848.

Institutes throughout the Province. In this way many earnest teachers who had received no training were given suggestions that bore much fruit.

When the Normal School was established, it was held in the old Legislative Buildings of Upper Canada. After the riots in Montreal, in 1849, Toronto again became the seat of Government and the Normal School had to move. Temporary quarters were obtained while the Council of Public Instruction took steps to secure a permanent home, not only for the Normal School, but for the Education Department. The present site was secured and Parliament made an appropriation of £15,000 to provide for it and for a building. In July, 1851, Lord Elgin laid the corner-stone.[118]

The address of Dr. Ryerson, in introducing the Governor, shows that he had no thought of divorcing the Common Schools from agriculture, the backbone industry of the people. He says: "The land on which these buildings are in course of erection is an entire square, consisting of nearly eight acres, two of which are to be devoted to a botanical garden, three to agricultural experiments, and the remainder to the buildings of the institution. It is thus intended that the valuable course of lectures given in the Normal School in vegetable physiology and agricultural chemistry shall be practically illustrated on the adjoining grounds, in the culture of which the students will take part during a portion of their hours of recreation. . . . There are four circumstances which encourage the most sanguine anticipations in every patriotic heart in regard to our educational future. The first is the avowed and entire absence of all party spirit in the school affairs of our country from the Provincial Legislature down to the smallest municipality. The second is the precedence which our Legislature has taken of all others on the western side of the Atlantic in providing for Normal School instruction, in aiding teachers to avail themselves of its advantages. The third is that the people of Upper Canada have during the last year voluntarily taxed themselves for the salaries of teachers in a larger sum in proportion to their numbers and have kept open their schools on an average more months than the neighbouring citizens of the old and great State of New York. The fourth is that the essential requisite of a series of suitable and excellent textbooks has been introduced into our schools and adopted almost by general acclamation, and that the facilities of furnishing all our schools with the necessary books, maps, and apparatus will soon be in advance of those of any other country."[119] In November, 1852, when the buildings[120] were formally opened, the Honourable John Beverley Robinson, Chief Justice of Upper Canada, said: "Without such a general preparatory system as we see here in operation, the instruction of the great mass of our population would be left in a measure to chance. The teachers might be, many of them, ignorant pretenders without experience, without method, and in some respects very improper persons to be entrusted with the education of youth. There could be little or no security for what they might teach, or what they might attempt to teach, nor any certainty that the good which might be acquired from their precepts would not be more than counterbalanced

[118] See D. H. E., Vol. X., pp. 5-14.

[119] See D. H. E., Vol. X., p. 6.

[120] These included what is now the main Departmental building and the Model School to the north. The present Normal School building was erected later.

by the ill effects of their example. Indeed the footing which our Common School teachers were formerly upon in regard to income gave no adequate remuneration to intelligent and industrious men to devote their time to the service. But this disadvantage is largely removed, as well as other obstacles which were inseparable from the conditions of a thinly-peopled and uncleared country traversed only by miserable roads, and henceforth, as soon at least as the benefits of this institution can be fully felt, the Common Schools will be dispensing throughout the whole of Upper Canada, by means of properly-trained teachers and under vigilant superintendents, a system of education which has been carefully considered and arranged, and which has been for some time practically exemplified. An observation of some years has enabled most of us to form an opinion of its sufficiency. Speaking only for myself, I have much pleasure in saying that the degree of proficiency which has been actually attained goes far, very far, beyond what I had imagined it would have been attempted to aim at."[121]

The following from Honourable Francis Hincks leaves us in no doubt as to Ryerson's part in securing the building. He says: "With regard to this institution, so far it has been most successfully conducted, and I feel bound to say that we must attribute all the merit of that success to the reverend gentleman who has been at the head of our Common School system. It is only due to him that I should take this public opportunity of saying that since I have been a member of the Government I have never met an individual who has displayed more zeal or more devotion to the duties he has been called upon to discharge than Dr. Ryerson. A great deal of opposition has been manifested both in and out of Parliament to this institution, and a good deal of jealousy exists with regard to its having been established in the city of Toronto. I can speak from my own experience as to the difficulties experienced in obtaining the co-operation of Parliament to have the necessary funds provided for the purpose of erecting this building. I will say, however, that there never was an institution in which the people have more confidence that the funds were well applied than in this institution. There is but one feeling that pervades the minds of all those who have seen the manner in which this scheme has been worked out. In regard to the Normal School itself, the site has been well chosen, the buildings have been erected in a most permanent manner, and without anything like extravagance, and I have no doubt there will be no difficulty in obtaining additional Parliamentary aid to finish them."[122]

In his report for 1853, Ryerson suggests Normal training for Grammar School teachers. I shall give his own words: "The Provincial Normal and Model Schools have contributed, and are contributing, much to the improvement of our Common Schools by furnishing a proper standard of judgment and comparison as to what such schools ought to be and how they should be taught and governed, and by furnishing teachers duly qualified for that important task. There is equal need of a Provincial Model Grammar School, in which the best modes of teaching the elements of Greek and Latin, French and German, the elementary mathematics and the elements of natural science, may be exemplified, and where teachers and candidates for masterships of Grammar Schools may have an opportunity

[121] See D. H. E., Vol. X., pp. 278-283.

[122] See D. H. E., Vol. X., pp. 282-284.

for practical observation and training during a shorter or longer period. Such a school would complete the educational establishments of our school system and contribute powerfully to advance Upper Canada to the proud position which she is approaching in regard to institutions and agencies for the mental culture of her youthful population."[123]

The Legislature voted £1,000 for a Model Grammar School, and in 1855 plans for a building were prepared under direction of the Council of Public Instruction. The estimate exceeded the means at the disposal of the Council and nothing was done until 1856, when Ryerson wrote the Executive Council as follows: "There is no branch of our system of Public Instruction so defective as our Grammar Schools, and the 'Model' for them as to both structure and furniture, discipline, modes of classification and teaching is of the utmost importance. . . . I am persuaded that a saving of one-half of the time and expense usually incurred in the Grammar School education of youth may be saved by improved methods in teaching and directing their studies, a result which will greatly increase the number of those who will aspire to a higher literary education apart from other advantages and intellectual habits and discipline. It is proposed to erect the Model Grammar School in the rear of the present Model School. . . . The proposed mode of admitting pupils will prevent the Model Grammar School from interfering with or being the rival of any other Grammar School. It is also intended to afford every possible facility and assistance to masters and teachers of Grammar Schools throughout the Province to come and spend some weeks in the Model Grammar School."[124]

The Government now authorized the Council of Public Instruction to proceed with the erection of a building to accommodate one hundred Grammar School pupils. The school was opened in 1858. It was the intention to give a preference to the two or three pupils from each county and city in Upper Canada who were recommended by the respective Municipal Councils. Ryerson's circular to these Councils will throw some light on the subject: "The object of the Model Grammar School is to exemplify the best methods of teaching the branches required by law to be taught in the Grammar Schools, especially the elementary classics and mathematics, as a model for the Grammar Schools of the country. It is also intended that the Model Grammar School shall, as far as possible, secure the advantages of a Normal Classical School to candidates for masterships in the Grammar School; but effect cannot be given to this object of the Model Grammar School during the first few months of its operation."[125] In 1859, in a report to the Government, Ryerson speaks further and says: "In regard to the Model Grammar Schools the buildings are completed and the school has been in operation several months and with the most gratifying success. Upwards of thirty masters of Grammar Schools have in the course of a few weeks visited and spent a longer or shorter time in the Model Grammar School with a view to improving their own methods of school organization, discipline, and teaching; and I have reason to believe that it has already exerted a salutary influence in improving the several Grammar Schools—an influence that will be greatly increased when we are enabled to form a special class

[123] See Superintendent's Report for 1853.

[124] See copy of letter in D. H. E., Vol. XII., p. 321.

[125] See copy of Circular in D. H. E., Vol. XIV., p. 65.

consisting of candidates for Grammar School masterships."[126]

In 1861, Mr. G. R. Cockburn, Rector of the Model Grammar School, resigned to become principal of Upper Canada College. Ryerson wished to transfer the functions of the Model Grammar School to Upper Canada College. This was not agreed to, but the same year provision was made for admitting candidates for Grammar School masterships to a course in training in the Model Grammar School. Up to this time the School had been of professional service as a school of observation, the holidays being so arranged that its classes were in session while Grammar School masters were on holiday.

In July, 1863, the Model Grammar School was finally closed. The following from a letter sent by Ryerson to the Provincial Secretary makes clear the reasons for this action: "When the Model Grammar School was established it was expected that nearly every county in Upper Canada would be represented in it and provision was made for that purpose. That important object has not been realized; and although the attendance at the school has been larger during the last year than during any previous year, reaching even to 100, the attendance as in former years has been chiefly from Toronto and its neighbourhood. I do not think it just to the General Fund to maintain an additional Toronto Grammar School. During the past year a training class for Grammar School masterships, consisting to a considerable extent of students in the University, has been successfully established. But it has been found that the instruction in all subjects, except Greek, Latin, and French, can be given in the Normal School to better advantage than in the Model Grammar School."[127]

Trained teachers for the Grammar Schools were much to be desired, and Ryerson deserves credit for his progressive ideas. But just at that stage in their evolution, although they contained many scholarly men, the Grammar Schools as a whole were more in need of teachers with sound scholarship than of teachers with a little professional training.

There continued to be complaints that teachers trained in the Normal Schools did not continue to teach. In his Report for 1856, Ryerson makes clear that in his opinion these defections from the teaching ranks were no condemnation of Normal Schools. He says: "The only objection yet made to the training of teachers, as far as I know, is that many of them do not pursue that profession but leave it for other employments. Were this true to the full extent imagined, the conclusion would still be in favour of the Normal School, since its advantages are not confined to schools or neighbourhoods in which its teachers are employed, but are extended over other neighbourhoods and municipalities. . . . In all professions and pursuits there are changes from one to another. I do not think it wise, just, or expedient to deny to the Normal School teacher the liberty, if opportunity presents itself, to improve his position or increase his usefulness. . . . In whatever position or relation of life a Normal School teacher may be placed, his training at the Normal School cannot fail to contribute to his usefulness."[128]

[126] See Report of Superintendent for 1859.
[127] See Ryerson's letter in D. H. E., Vol. XVIII, p. 69.
[128] See Report of Chief Superintendent for 1856. See copy in D. H. E., Vol. XIII., p. 51.

Nor was all the criticism of Normal School affairs directed towards the teachers who left the profession; those who remained in it were emissaries of evil. Then, as now, there were croakers who thought that a boy born on a farm naturally belonged there, and that any enlightenment which tended to make him dissatisfied with his surroundings was an evil. One, signing himself Angus Dallas of Toronto, wrote several pamphlets attacking the school system. Speaking of the Normal School, he said: "The young men who have attended six months at that institution and leave it with certificates to teach, go forth into the country with the most mistaken estimate of their own importance. They open schools wherever accident places them, and by teaching and familiar intercourse, combined with the example of nomadic habits, for they seldom remain longer than twelve months in one place, they soon contaminate the minds of the older pupils and also of young men who may reside in the neighbourhood, by their doctrines of enlightened citizenship; and thus these pupils soon learn to disdain honest labour."[129]

In 1855, the Legislature had authorized a museum and library in connection with the Department of Education. These were formally opened in 1857 and the library contributed much to increase the efficiency of the Normal School by widening the scope of the students' reading.

In the following year the Council of Public Instruction revised the Normal School Regulations. Qualifications necessary for admission were accurately set forth and the course of study defined for both second and first-class certificates. There continued to be two sessions a year, but students who entered to qualify for a second-class certificate spent two or more sessions before reaching a standard entitling them to a first-class certificate.

An interesting sidelight is thrown upon the nature of the instruction given in the Toronto Normal School by the Report for 1868 of George Paxton Young, Inspector of Grammar Schools. Young was trying to raise the standard of the Grammar Schools, and shows how their improvement would affect the Normal Schools. He says: "I suppose there can be no doubt that if High Schools like those which I have described were established, it would be necessary to modify the work of the Normal School considerably. Teachers who would have to perform different duties from what have hitherto been expected at their hands would need a different training from what has hitherto been given. The instructions in English in the Normal School would require to be raised to a far higher level than is now aimed at. Much of the elementary drilling which Normal School students at present receive might be dispensed with. Our institution for the training of teachers ought not to be a school for teaching English grammar. In the same way I would lighten the ship of such subjects as the bare facts of geography and history; not rejecting of course prelections on the proper method of teaching geography and history. The English master in the Normal School might thus be enabled to devote a portion of his time to lessons in the English language and literature of a superior cast—

[129] The Toronto schools were at this time very expensively managed as compared with schools in other cities of Upper Canada. This could not be attributed to the expense of Normal-trained teachers. In 1858, ten years after the Normal School was established, no Common School in Toronto was in charge of a Normal-trained teacher, and only two or three such teachers had ever been employed there. See D. H. E., Vol. XIII., p. 299.

lessons which he would have a pride in giving and on which the students would feel it a privilege to wait. Such lessons would be immensely useful even to those young men and women who might only desire to qualify themselves for becoming Common School teachers. In the department of physical science, it is plain that if the views which I have expressed in regard to the way in which science should be taught in the High Schools be just, the object of the prelections in the Normal School should not be to cram the students with a mass of facts but to develop in them a philosophic habit of mind and to make them practically understand how classes in science ought to be conducted in the schools."[130]

No man in Canada was better qualified to estimate the real work of any educational establishment than Young, and although he was not closely connected with the Normal School, we may assume that his analysis was essentially correct and that the study of formal grammar and the acquisition of scientific facts bulked large in the Normal School programme. In his report for 1867,[131] in speaking of the Normal and Model Schools, Ryerson says: "They are not constituted as are most of the Normal Schools in both Europe and America to impart the preliminary education requisite for teaching. That preparatory education is supposed to have been attained in the ordinary public or private schools. The entrance examination to the Normal School requires this. The object of the Normal and Model Schools is, therefore, to do for the teacher what an apprenticeship does for the mechanic, the artist, the physician, the lawyer—to teach him theoretically and practically how to do the work of his profession."

A little consideration will show us that a school trying to realize such an aim and attempting to teach only the rudiments of the science of education, upon which the theory of teaching is based, must become empirical and rule-of-thumb in its methods. The real difficulty lay in the inadequate preparation with which the teachers in training entered upon their work. The Normal School could not improve until an improvement should be effected in the Grammar Schools.

During the first nine sessions of the Normal School no certificates were granted which entitled the holder to teach. The Normal School graduates simply received certificates of attendance and had to submit to examination by a County Board before securing a license. It almost invariably happened that Normal School graduates were able to take a high standing at these examinations, and hence Ryerson met with no serious opposition from County Boards when in 1853 he proposed to issue Provincial certificates to Normal School graduates upon the recommendation of the Normal School masters. From 1853 to 1871 a dual system of granting certificates was in operation. Normal School graduates received Provincial certificates of various grades, and County Boards issued certificates valid only in the county where issued. In 1871 a radical change was made, by which County Boards were allowed to issue only third-class certificates valid for three years in the county where given, and renewable on the recommendation of the County Inspector. Second and first-class certificates were granted only by the Department of Education and valid during good behaviour, and in any part of the Province. A first-class

[130] See D. H. E., Vol. XX., p. 127.
[131] See D. H. E., Vol. XX., p. 139.

certificate of the highest grade (Grade "A") was made the qualification for County Inspectors. It should also be noted that the third-class certificates referred to above were granted after 1871 only upon the passing of a written examination upon papers prepared by a central committee chosen by the Council of Public Instruction. This was a radical change from the old method, which allowed each County Board to fix its own standard, a plan which necessarily led to many certificates being granted to wholly incompetent persons.

The change of 1871, which virtually established a Provincial system of licensing teachers, brought upon Ryerson's head much abuse from incompetent teachers and their friends. The Superintendent stood firmly by his guns, knowing well that his act was in the best interests of the Province. A few words from his reply to those who objected that old teachers were being set aside because of failure to pass the Provincial examination is worth mentioning. He says: "I answer, as government exists not for office-holders but for the people, so the school exists not for the teachers but for the youth and future generations of the land; and if teachers have been too slothful not to keep pace with the progressive wants and demands of the country, they must, as should all incompetent and indolent public officers, and all lazy and unenterprising citizens, give place to the more industrious, intelligent, progressive, and enterprising. The sound education of a generation of children is not to be sacrificed for the sake of an incompetent although antiquated teacher."[132]

Having secured the adoption of a system by which all licensing of teachers was under Departmental control, Ryerson next turned his attention to an extension of facilities for training teachers. His plans were comprehensive and had to wait thirty-five years for complete realization. In 1872[133] he reported to the Provincial Treasurer as follows: "I desire to state in reply that last year I thought and suggested to the Government that two additional Normal Schools were required, one in the eastern and the other in the western section of the Province, but I am now inclined to think that three additional Normal Schools will be required to extend the advantages of a Normal School training to all parts of the Province—one at London, one at Kingston, and one at Ottawa. If provision be not made to establish them all at once, I think the first established should be at Ottawa—the centre of a large region of country where the schools are in a comparatively backward state, and where the influence of the Normal School training for teachers has yet been scarcely felt except in a few towns, and which is almost entirely separated from Toronto in all branches of business and commerce, and therefore, to a great extent, in social relations and sympathies. . . . As the whole Province east of Belleville is less advanced and less progressive in schools than the western parts, I think a second Normal School should be established at Kingston. The whole region of country from Belleville, on the west, to Brockville, on the east, has very little more business or commercial connection with Toronto than the more eastern parts of the Province. Although London is not so remote from Toronto as Ottawa or Kingston, yet it is the centre of a populous and prosperous part of the Province from which an ample number of student teachers would be collected to fill any

[132] See copy of Report in D. H. E., Vol. XIII., p. 131.

[133] See D. H. E., Vol. XXIV., p. 22.

Normal School. . . . With the establishment of these three Normal Schools I am persuaded there would still be as large a number of student teachers attending the Toronto School as can advantageously be trained in one institution. . . . I think all the Normal Schools should be subject to the oversight of the Education Department and under the same regulations formally sanctioned by the Lieutenant-Governor-in-Council. This I think necessary on the grounds of both economy and uniformity of standard and system of instruction. As to the extent of accommodation in each Normal School, I think that provision should be made for training 150 teachers in each school."

In the meantime, while negotiations for more Normal School accommodation were in progress, an attempt was made to give some professional training through teachers' institutes. As far back as 1850 the Legislature had made a grant for such meetings, and they had been conducted by the Normal School masters. In 1872 the plan was revised and some very successful institutes held. The movement is important because out of it grew County Model Schools, and the adoption of a principle which meant some professional training for every teacher.

In 1875, a Normal School was opened at Ottawa, but the plan of having schools at Kingston and London was abandoned largely because of the apathy of the Legislature in regard to the expense. In fact it is doubtful if any Government could have forced through the Legislature a vote for such a purpose.

Ryerson found the schools in 1844 taught by teachers without certificates and without professional training; he left them in 1876 with teachers, all of whom were certificated under Government examinations, and many of whom were Normal-trained. More important still, he had, by his lectures at County Conventions and by his writings in the *Journal of Education,* created a sentiment throughout the Province in favour of trained teachers. He thus made easy the pathway of his successors in securing increased efficiency; but it may be doubted whether any of his immediate successors achieved results in keeping with the material advance of the Province.

CHAPTER XI.

RYERSON SCHOOL BILL OF 1871.

From 1850 to 1871 no wholly new principles relating to the Common Schools were adopted by the Legislature, although some changes were necessarily made. The legislation of 1850 had, from time to time, to be supplemented by amendments in order that the spirit of the previous legislation should be made applicable to the needs of a rapidly growing community.

An Act passed in 1853[134] provided further machinery for the working of Trustee Boards; gave a liberal annual grant for an educational museum; set apart £500 a year toward teachers' pensions, and increased by £1,000 a year the grant to Normal Schools.

An Act passed in 1860[135] more clearly defined the powers of trustees, the manner of conducting elections, and auditing school accounts. The same Act made Saturday a school holiday.

The Act of 1871[136] was the last important school legislation prepared by Ryerson.[137] The important features of the Act may be summed up under four headings, viz., compulsory and free education, efficient inspection, teachers' pensions, and the licensing of teachers under Government direction.[138]

The free school was the natural complement of the Act of 1850. The permissive legislation then enacted allowing trustee boards and ratepayers to establish free schools had been so generally acted upon[139] that by 1871 the abolition of all rate bills upon parents seemed to come as a matter of course. The logical corollary of free schools is compulsory attendance, and the Act of 1871 fixed penalties to be imposed upon parents and guardians who neglected the education of their children. It may be doubted whether this compulsory clause has ever been of any real advantage to the cause of education. The real forces that move human beings are always moral forces. Many a man has unwillingly sent his children to school because of public opinion, but few because of fear of the law.

[134] See copy of Act reprinted in D. H. E., Vol. X., p. 133.

[135] See copy of Act reprinted in D. H. E., Vol. XV., pp. 45-49.

[136] See copy of Act reprinted in D. H. E., Vol. XXII., pp. 213-222.

[137] The Act of 1874, in as far as it contained new principles, was forced upon Ryerson by the Government of Sir Oliver Mowat.

[138] For changes made in Grammar Schools by Act of 1871, see Chapter IX.

[139] Only some 400 schools out of 4,000 were levying rate bills in 1870. These 400 were chiefly in towns and cities. The total rate bill levy for 1870 was about $24,000. See Superintendent's Report for 1870.

The Act provided for county inspectors who should be experts and devote their whole time to the work of inspection. Ryerson's first Report had foreshadowed such action, and the fact that he had to wait a quarter-century to realize his plan shows how impossible it is to legislate much in advance of public opinion.

The County Inspector, together with two or more qualified teachers, were to form a County Board, with power to license second and third-class teachers upon examinations prescribed by the Council of Public Instruction. In this way the Superintendent had at last secured a uniform standard of qualification for teachers throughout the whole Province.

The small annual grant made for teachers' pensions in 1853, and increased a few years later to $4,000 per annum, had enabled the Superintendent to dole out pittances[140] to a few score of worn-out teachers whose need was most pressing. Ryerson wished to establish a system such as was in operation in Germany—a system of compulsory payments by teachers in service sufficient to give a substantial pension for old age. He hoped by this means to secure a body of teachers with a professional spirit, and to enable them to spend their declining years in independence.

The Act of 1871 required compulsory payments from male teachers of four dollars per year.[141] At a later date County Inspectors and all first-class teachers were required to pay six dollars a year. This payment guaranteed an annual pension upon retirement of four or six dollars for every year's contribution. Female teachers were allowed, but not forced, to support the Pension Fund. The compulsory payments aroused much opposition from some teachers, especially those who were making temporary use of the teachers' calling as a stepping-stone to some other profession.[142] Ryerson thought that this class might very properly be taxed a trifle for the general cause of education.

Minor provisions of the Act of 1871 gave trustee boards power to build teachers' residences and to secure land for school sites by arbitration. The Act also authorized the creation of Township Boards of Trustees, where public opinion favoured them.

During its passage through the Legislature the Bill of 1871 was severely criticized by Hon. George Brown, in the Toronto *Globe*, and by Edward Blake, on the floor of the Assembly. Perhaps neither of these gentlemen had any love for Ryerson, but they represented a new spirit which Ryerson scarcely understood, and with which he certainly had no sympathy.

Mr. Blake opposed the Bill upon several grounds, but especially upon the abolition of rate bills and the irresponsible nature of the Council of Public Instruction. As regards the former he expressed himself heartily in favour of free schools, but

[140] See D. H. E., Vol. XX., p. 143.

[141] No doubt this seems a ridiculously small contribution, but we must remember that teachers received very small salaries. The Pension Fund clause was repealed in 1885 on request of the teachers of Ontario, and since that date no names have been added to the list. The payments by teachers provided only a small proportion of the annual charge upon the Pension Fund. The present annual charge (1910) upon the Fund is $55,926.

[142] See D. H. E., Vol. XXIII., pp. 253-256.

since they were gradually becoming free without compulsion he wished to let them alone. His objection to the Council of Public Instruction[143] is worthy of note because it brings out in a strong light the real bone of contention between Ryerson and the Ontario Liberals, and enables us to understand why at a later date it was impossible for Ryerson to work in harmony with a Liberal Executive Council. The Council of Public Instruction was an irresponsible body appointed by the Crown and dominated by the Chief Superintendent. It had extensive powers. It might act arbitrarily, and yet there was no way by which the members of the Legislature could call it to account or insist upon explanations. Mr. Blake and his colleagues argued that this was not compatible with representative government. Doctor Ryerson insisted that the Education Department must be wholly removed from party politics. Conscious of purity of purpose and personal integrity, he was ever more desirous of giving the people what he thought they needed than of giving them what they wanted.

Although Ryerson had taken a partisan's part in politics before his appointment as Superintendent, he wisely tried to administer his Department upon a non-partisan basis. And he met with a large measure of success because all sensible men realized that education ought not to be a topic for partisan bickerings. For many years it was so arranged that the leader of the Government introduced educational bills and the leader of the Opposition seconded them.

Such a procedure was possible only so long as both political parties had more confidence in the wisdom of the Superintendent to deal with education than they had in the educational foresight of their own leaders. But such a confidence could not be indefinitely retained by any Superintendent, and certainly not by Ryerson, who was very sensitive to criticism of his administration, and always ready to challenge any layman who had the temerity to express an opinion upon education contrary to his. It was inevitable that a clash should come, and it was a great tribute to Ryerson's wisdom in gauging public opinion that the clash was so long delayed. It was also quite to be expected that the Liberal leaders should be the ones to precipitate the shock, seeing that Ryerson had ridden into office upon a wave of Tory reaction.

Mr. Blake and Hon. George Brown could, however, make little headway against Ryerson in connection with the School Bill of 1871. Except in regard to the irresponsible nature of the Council of Public Instruction, the Act was progressive and truly liberal. Ryerson had discussed every clause in the Bill at County Conventions, and had behind him the support of all actively engaged in the work of education and in the other learned professions.

---

[143] See Pamphlet in Parliamentary Library, Ottawa, addressed by Edward Blake to the electors of South Bruce.

CHAPTER XII.

CONCLUSION.

How are we to sum up the work of this man who moulded the schools of Ontario during a period as long as the life of a single generation? Would the schools of 1876 have been what they were had there been no Ryerson? We think not.

No doubt the people of Upper Canada would, without Ryerson, have worked out a good school system, because a school system must in the end reflect the average intelligence and the fixed ideals of a people. But in Ryerson, Upper Canada had a man who, by his dogged determination and his hold upon the affections of the people, was able to secure legislation somewhat in advance of a fixed public opinion. To a considerable extent he created the public sentiment which made his work possible. He knew what the people needed and persuaded them to accept it. This we conceive to be the work of a statesman.

Ryerson was neither a demagogue nor a constitutionalist. He had none of the arts of one who wins the populace by flattering its vanity. He was too sincere and too deeply religious to appeal to the lower springs of human action. On the other hand he had no real sympathy with popular government. He would let people do as they wished, only so long as they wished to do what he believed to be right. He never could believe that he himself might be wrong. Even had he wished to do so, he never could have divested himself wholly of the character of priest and pedagogue. He was always either shouting from the pulpit or thumping the desk of the schoolmaster.

His environment after 1844 strengthened and developed his natural tendency to be autocratic. He worked like a giant. He created the Education Department, appointed his subordinates, was his own finance minister, established a Normal School and appointed its instructors, nominated members of a Council of Public Instruction who often did little more than formally register his decrees, organized a book and map depository and an educational museum, edited an educational journal in which he published his decrees, and prepared legislation for successive Legislatures having comparatively few members competent to criticize school administration. He administered one of the largest spending Departments of Government, and ruled somewhat rigorously a score of subordinates, and yet, for many years, was not subject to any check except the nominal one of the Governor-General, and later of the Governor-General-in-Council.

When he visited District or County Conventions he came as a lawgiver, either to explain existing regulations, promulgate new ones, or obtain assent to those for which he wished to secure legislation. Only after the Grammar Schools had become efficient did Ryerson meet at Teachers' Conventions men who were intellectually his equals and who were ready to criticize his policy, and, when necessary, give him wholesome advice. Had Ryerson been a responsible Minister with a seat in the Legislature, either his nature would have been modified or he would have failed, probably the latter.

This would seem to lead to the conclusion that Ryerson after all was not a statesman, since a statesman must, in our age, carry out his measures and at the same time retain the confidence of his colleagues and the electors. But this is just what Ryerson did, although he did not do it directly through the Legislature. He appealed to a Court beyond the Legislature—the whole body of intelligent men and women of Upper Canada—and this Court sustained him in his work for thirty-two years, during which time it is doubtful if any single constituency in the country would have elected him to two successive Parliaments. If this be true we may safely assume that it was a happy chance which gave us a non-political Education Department during our formative period.

Ryerson's greatest admirers can scarcely claim that he was a scholar. This was his misfortune and not his fault. He never failed to embrace whatever opportunities for intellectual improvement came in his way. His reading of history was broad and discriminating. He had little interest in anything that did not bear somewhat directly upon the problem of human virtue. Consequently his interests centred largely in civil government and theology.

Nor can we claim for Ryerson that he introduced original legislation. Hardly anything in our system of education was of his invention. New England, New York, Germany, and Ireland gave him his models, and his genius was shown in the skill with which he adapted these to suit the needs of Upper Canada. Even in the details of his school legislation, especially that relating to High Schools, Ryerson adopted suggestions of men more competent than himself to form a judgment. To say this in no way detracts from the man's greatness. Little after all in modern legislation is actually new, and to say of a man that he is successful in using other men's ideas is often to give him the highest praise.

In one department of work Ryerson stood in a class by himself. He was without a peer as an administrator. His intensely practical mind was quick to discover the shortest route between end and means. His energy, his system and attention to details, his broad personal knowledge of actual conditions, his capacity for long periods of effort, his thrift, his courteous treatment of subordinates, and even his sensitiveness to criticism were factors which enabled him to administer the most difficult Department of the Government with ease and smoothness.

The history of Upper Canada during a period of nearly sixty years is as much bound up with the labours of Egerton Ryerson as with the work of any other public man. He gave us lofty ideals of the meaning and purpose of life, and he had an abiding faith in the power of popular education to aid in a realization of these ideals; he fought for free schools in Upper Canada when they needed a valiant champion. Let the present generation of men and women honour the memory of the man who wrought so faithfully for their fathers and grandfathers.

BIBLIOGRAPHY.

Documentary History of Education in Upper Canada. 28 vols. Dr. J. Geo. Hodgins.

Story of My Life. Egerton Ryerson. Edited by Dr. J. Geo. Hodgins.

Egerton Ryerson. Chancellor Burwash.

Loyalists of America. 2 vols. Egerton Ryerson.

Ryerson Memorial Volume. Edited by Dr. J. Geo. Hodgins.

History of Upper Canada College. Principal Dickson.

Journals of Assembly of Upper Canada, Legislative Library, Toronto.

Journal of Education, 1848-1876. 29 vols. Library of Parliament, Ottawa.

Ryerson's Special Reports on European Schools. Library of Parliament, Ottawa.

Ryerson's Annual School Reports, 1845-1876. Library of Parliament, Ottawa.

Gourlay's Statistical Account of Upper Canada. 3 vols. Published by Simpkins and Marshall, London, Eng., 1822.

Sketches of Canada and the United States. William Lyon Mackenzie. Published by Effingham & Wilson, London, Eng., 1833.

Reminiscences of His Public Life. Sir Francis Hincks.

Ryerson's Controversy with Rev. J. M. Bruyère on Free Schools. Canadian Pamphlets, vol. 50. Library of Parliament, Ottawa.

Ryerson's Letters to Doctor Strachan, on Education. Canadian Pamphlets, vol. 83.

Ryerson's New Canadian Dominion. Canadian Pamphlets, vol. 418.

Ryerson's Defence Against Attacks of Hon. George Brown. Canadian Pamphlets, vol. 418.

Ryerson on the Separate School Law of Upper Canada. Canadian Pamphlets, vol. 416.

Ryerson on a Liberal Education in Upper Canada. Canadian Pamphlets, vol. 416.

Ryerson on the School Book Question. Canadian Pamphlets, vol. 416.

Ryerson, a Review and a Study. J. A. Allen. Canadian Pamphlets, vol. 667.

Bishop Strachan, a Review and a Study. Rev. Doctor Scadding. Canadian Pamphlets, vol. 169.

Report on Grievances in Upper Canada. William Lyon Mackenzie. Library of Parliament, Ottawa.

Bound Volumes of Toronto *Globe*, 1844-1876, in Legislative Library, Toronto.

British Colonist. Published by H. Scobie, 1838-1854. Library of Parliament, Ottawa.

Kingston Chronicle and Gazette, 1840-1842. Library of Parliament, Ottawa.

Courier of Upper Canada, 1836-1837. Library of Parliament, Ottawa.

Weekly Colonist, 1852-1855. Library of Parliament, Ottawa.

Ryerson's Correspondence with Provincial Secretaries, 1844-1876. Canadian Archives, Ottawa.

Printed by Libri Plureos GmbH in Hamburg,
Germany

9 789361 388286